D1309628

XXXIV International Biennial Exhibition of Art, Venice, Italy, 1968: United States of America

An exhibition selected by Norman A. Geske, Director,
University of Nebraska Art Galleries, Lincoln, Nebraska

Organized by the International Art Program,
National Collection of Fine Arts,
Smithsonian Institution, Washington, D.C.

Commissioner-at-Large, Norman A. Geske

Commissioner, Lois A. Bingham, Chief, International Art Program,
National Collection of Fine Arts

Deputy Commissioner, Margaret Cogswell, Deputy Chief, International Art Program,
National Collection of Fine Arts

Exhibition Architect, Charles Forberg

Assistants to the Commissioner: Mrs. Marietta Stern-Guetta, Mrs. James Smith Bush

Pavilion Curator, Jonathan Scull

United States Pavilion, Venice, Italy,
June 22–October 20, 1968

National Collection of Fine Arts, Washington, D.C.
December 19, 1968–February 2, 1969

Sheldon Memorial Art Gallery, University of Nebraska, Lincoln, Nebraska,
March 17–April 13, 1969

VENICE 34

The Figurative Tradition in Recent American Art

by NORMAN A. GESKE

Published for the National Collection of Fine Arts
by the Smithsonian Institution Press
Washington, D.C.

709.73
G389
N 6512
G4

Copyright © 1968, Smithsonian Institution, Washington, D.C.
Library of Congress Catalog Card No. 68–61295
Designed by Dwight Stark
Composition, printing and binding by Clarke & Way, Inc., New York
Printed in the United States of America

The Smithsonian Institution is once again pleased to present a compelling and diverse American entry in the *XXXIV Esposizione Biennale Internazionale d'Arte.*

Through the years these great biennial exhibitions—and companion international shows elsewhere—present a striking and meaningful panoramic view of artistic creativity throughout the world.

They speak eloquently of art and artists, and accordingly of men and nations. Just as the artist makes an important contribution to each of us as individuals, these major exhibitions benefit us all even as they stimulate and encourage painters and sculptors in all of the participating countries.

By focusing on the figurative tradition in recent American art, this exhibit of painting and sculpture by ten American entrants also looks searchingly at man, a traditional study for the artist that today is perhaps more important than ever before to all men.

I think it is notable that the University of Nebraska, which joined with the National Collection of Fine Arts of the Smithsonian Institution in organizing this American exhibition, is now concluding 100 years as an educational institution that has devoted considerable attention through the years to art and art education. We are grateful to the University of Nebraska and proud of both its Sheldon Memorial Art Gallery and the Venice 1968 show that it was instrumental in selecting.

S. Dillon Ripley
Secretary, Smithsonian Institution

America's creative centers are widespread geographically and varied in nature. This is one of the great sources of strength for our national culture, and one which is reflected in this year's exhibition. Mr. Norman Geske, our Commissioner-at-Large, is the director of the art gallery of the university of a primarily agricultural state some 1500 miles from New York or Washington. Yet his concerns are by no means regional: his perspectives are carefully balanced. He has with great catholicity worked out the rationale and made the selections for a freshly-conceived, revealing exhibition, one which should add significantly to the understanding of contemporary American art when it is placed on the international stage.

The National Collection of Fine Arts is most happy to have the privilege of cosponsoring this exhibition with the Sheldon Memorial Art Gallery of the University of Nebraska, and we wish to express our appreciation to Mr. Geske for his dedicated, constructive efforts in behalf of American art.

David W. Scott
Director, National Collection of Fine Arts

In 1969 the University of Nebraska will celebrate its Centennial. It has been committed to the teaching of art for 92 of these first 100 years; and for 78 of these years its commitment has been to acquire and exhibit contemporary American art, in collaboration with the Nebraska Art Association. The University is especially proud of the Sheldon Memorial Art Gallery and its notable collections which are fulfilling this commitment.

The Smithsonian Institution's invitation to organize the American exhibition at the XXXIV Biennale is one that the University of Nebraska accepts with pleasure as a particularly apt, although coincidental, commemoration of its Centennial.

JUL 17 1970

Clifford M. Hardin
Chancellor, University of Nebraska

The presentation of the American exhibition at the XXXIV Biennale has been made possible by the generous support of many individuals, foundations and corporations. We would like to express our deep appreciation of their help in this important project.

Mr. and Mrs. Richard Agee, Lincoln, Nebraska
Mr. and Mrs. Martin I. Aitken, Lincoln, Nebraska
Mr. and Mrs. John H. Ames, Lincoln, Nebraska
Mr. and Mrs. A. Douglas Anderson, Lincoln, Nebraska
Dr. and Mrs. Everett E. Angle, Lincoln, Nebraska
Mr. and Mrs. John C. Angle, Lincoln, Nebraska
Mr. and Mrs. Fred Arnold, Lincoln, Nebraska
Mrs. Winifred Arnold, Lincoln, Nebraska
Mrs. Dorothy Ayers, Lexington, Nebraska
Mrs. Henry S. Barshinger, Lincoln, Nebraska
Mr. and Mrs. Walter D. Behlen, Columbus, Nebraska
Mr. and Mrs. Forrest E. Behm, Jr., Corning, New York
Mrs. B. C. Biggs, Lincoln, Nebraska
Miss Barbara Birmingham, O'Neill, Nebraska
Dr. and Mrs. James D. Bisgard, Omaha, Nebraska
Mr. and Mrs. James S. Blackman, Lincoln, Nebraska
Mr. and Mrs. Cecil Carstenson, Kansas City, Missouri
Mr. and Mrs. Thomas P. Coleman, Lincoln, Nebraska
Mr. and Mrs. George B. Cook, Lincoln, Nebraska
Mr. and Mrs. N. H. Cromwell, Lincoln, Nebraska
Mr. and Mrs. Philip A. Crowl, Lincoln, Nebraska
Mr. and Mrs. Thomas M. Davies, Lincoln, Nebraska
Mrs. Herbert Davis, Omaha, Nebraska
Mrs. Stephen D. Day, Lincoln, Nebraska
Mrs. Wentworth Dodge, Omaha, Nebraska
Mr. and Mrs. David Dow, Lincoln, Nebraska
Dr. and Mrs. Harold E. Edgerton, Cambridge, Massachusetts
Mr. and Mrs. James Eisentrager, Lincoln, Nebraska
Mr. and Mrs. L. A. Enersen, Lincoln, Nebraska
Mr. and Mrs. E. J. Faulkner, Lincoln, Nebraska
Mr. and Mrs. Arnott R. Folsom, Lincoln, Nebraska
Mrs. Willard M. Folsom, Lincoln, Nebraska
Mrs. Elsie G. Fullerton, Lincoln, Nebraska
Dr. and Mrs. Richard E. Garlinghouse, Lincoln, Nebraska
Mr. and Mrs. Ray E. George, Lincoln, Nebraska
Dr. and Mrs. Paul Goetowski, Lincoln, Nebraska
Mr. and Mrs. Bernard Gradwohl, Lincoln, Nebraska
Mr. and Mrs. Richard H. Greenburg, San Francisco, California
Mr. and Mrs. J. Taylor Greer, Lincoln, Nebraska
Dr. and Mrs. Walter E. Hager, Bethesda, Maryland
Mrs. Helen J. Haggie, Lincoln, Nebraska
Mr. and Mrs. Robert S. Haller, Lincoln, Nebraska
Mr. and Mrs. Robert E. Henderson, Lincoln, Nebraska
Mr. and Mrs. Lyle C. Holland, Lincoln, Nebraska
Senator Calista Cooper Hughes and Mr. Morris N. Hughes, Humboldt, Nebraska
Miss Laura Ingham, Lincoln, Nebraska
Dr. and Mrs. Ralph L. Ireland, Lincoln, Nebraska

Mr. Merle S. Jones, New York, New York
Mr. Oliver T. Joy, Lincoln, Nebraska
Mr. and Mrs. Howard Kaplan, Omaha, Nebraska
Mr. and Mrs. Curtis D. Kimball, Lincoln, Nebraska
Mr. and Mrs. Eugene Kingman, Omaha, Nebraska
Senator and Mrs. Albert Kjar, Lexington, Nebraska
Miss Shirley M. Kreutz, Lincoln, Nebraska
Mr. and Mrs. George Legeros, Minneapolis, Minnesota
Rev. and Mrs. Anton W. Loock, Lexington, Nebraska
Mr. Ralph R. Lounsbury, Montclair, New Jersey
Miss Elva L. McFie, Lincoln, Nebraska
Mr. Ephraim L. Marks, Omaha, Nebraska
Mr. and Mrs. Corwin D. Moore, Lincoln, Nebraska
Mrs. Elizabeth B. Mueller, Lincoln, Nebraska
Miss Louise A. Nixon, Lincoln, Nebraska
Mr. and Mrs. A. Craig O'Brien, Lincoln, Nebraska
Mr. and Mrs. James C. Olson, Lincoln, Nebraska
Mrs. Carl Olson, Lincoln, Nebraska
Dr. Janet F. Palmer, Lincoln, Nebraska
Mr. and Mrs. Thomas R. Pansing, Lincoln, Nebraska
Miss Jane L. Pope, Lincoln, Nebraska
Mr. and Mrs. James Rawley, Lincoln, Nebraska
Mrs. Waunita W. Ray, Lincoln, Nebraska
Mr. and Mrs. Lawrence Reger, Lincoln, Nebraska
Mr. David M. Rice, Omaha, Nebraska
Dr. and Mrs. Vance D. Rogers, Lincoln, Nebraska
Mr. and Mrs. C. H. Rohman, Lincoln, Nebraska
Mrs. Mary Riepma Ross, New York, New York
Mr. and Mrs. J. R. Seacrest, Lincoln, Nebraska
Mr. and Mrs. David W. Seyler, Lincoln, Nebraska
Mrs. A. B. Sheldon, Lexington, Nebraska
Mr. and Mrs. Frank Sidles, Lincoln, Nebraska
Mr. and Mrs. Richard W. Smith, Lincoln, Nebraska
Mr. and Mrs. Louis Sosland, Shawnee Mission, Kansas
Mrs. Freda N. Spaulding, Lincoln, Nebraska
Mrs. Albert Speier, Lincoln, Nebraska
Mr. and Mrs. Robert Spence, Lincoln, Nebraska
Mr. and Mrs. K. E. Staley, Boca Raton, Florida
Dr. and Mrs. Edmund A. Steenburg, Aurora, Nebraska
Mrs. Olga Stepanek, Lincoln, Nebraska
Dr. and Mrs. Lee Stover, Lincoln, Nebraska
Mr. and Mrs. Eugene R. Tait, Lincoln, Nebraska
Mrs. Vernon L. Thompson, Lincoln, Nebraska
Governor and Mrs. Norbert T. Tiemann, Lincoln, Nebraska
Mr. and Mrs. Richard Trickey, Lincoln Nebraska
Miss Agnes Van Ackeren, Lincoln, Nebraska
Mrs. Mary D. Vogel, Omaha, Nebraska
Mr. Harry L. Weaver, Lincoln, Nebraska
Mr. and Mrs. Fred N. Wells, Lincoln, Nebraska
Mr. and Mrs. Walter W. White, Lincoln, Nebraska

Mr. and Mrs. Emanuel Wishnow, Lincoln, Nebraska
Mr. and Mrs. Frank H. Woods, Chicago, Illinois
Mr. and Mrs. Thomas C. Woods, Jr., Lincoln,
 Nebraska
Mr. and Mrs. Morley Zipursky, Omaha, Nebraska

Abel Foundation, Lincoln, Nebraska
Association of Nebraska Art Clubs
Behlen Bros. Mfg. Co., Columbus, Nebraska
Central National Insurance Group of Omaha,
 Omaha, Nebraska
Community Savings Stamp Co., Lincoln, Nebraska
Leo A. Daly Company, Omaha, Nebraska
Doane College, Crete, Nebraska
Dobson Brothers Construction Co., Lincoln,
 Nebraska
Dorsey Laboratories, Lincoln, Nebraska
Fairmont Foods Company, Omaha, Nebraska
First National Bank and Trust Co., Lincoln, Nebraska
Gallagher Foundation, Omaha, Nebraska
Guarantee Mutual Life Insurance Co., Omaha,
 Nebraska
Henningson, Durham & Richardson, Omaha,
 Nebraska
Kansas-Nebraska Natural Gas Co., Inc.,
 Hastings, Nebraska
L & M Enterprises, Inc., Lincoln, Nebraska

Lincoln Artists' Guild, Lincoln, Nebraska
Lincoln Chamber of Commerce, Lincoln, Nebraska
Lincoln Foundation, Inc., Lincoln, Nebraska
National Bank of Commerce Trust
 and Savings Association, Lincoln, Nebraska
Nebraska Art Association, Lincoln, Nebraska
Nebraska Art Teachers' Association
Nebraska Consolidated Mills Co., Omaha, Nebraska
Nebraska-Iowa Chapter, American Institute of
 Designers, Omaha, Nebraska
Northwestern Bell Telephone Co., Omaha,
 Nebraska
Omaha Art Guild No. 2, Omaha, Nebraska
Omaha Art Guild No. 7, Omaha, Nebraska
Omaha Art Guild No. 8, Omaha, Nebraska
The Omaha National Bank, Omaha, Nebraska
Pontiac Division—General Motors Corporation
Sidles RCA Appliances, Omaha, Nebraska
Carl and Caroline Swanson Foundation, Omaha,
 Nebraska
Tuesday Review Club, Lincoln, Nebraska
United States National Bank, Omaha, Nebraska
Vanice Pontiac-Cadillac, Inc., Lincoln, Nebraska
Western Power & Gas Company,
 Lincoln, Nebraska
Wilson and Company, Chicago, Illinois
Woods Charitable Fund, Inc., Chicago, Illinois

Lenders to the Exhibition

Mr. and Mrs. Robert Baldwin, Nashville,
 Tennessee
Mr. and Mrs. Douglass Boshkoff, Bloomington,
 Indiana
Mr. Edwin Constant Dickinson, Tokyo, Japan
Dr. and Mrs. James Jay, New York
Mr. and Mrs. Gardner Jencks, New York
Mrs. Constant Jewett, New York
Mr. and Mrs. Leonard Lauder, New York
Mr. Wade Perry, New Haven, Connecticut
Mrs. Katherine White Reswick, Cleveland, Ohio
Mr. and Mrs. Robert Robles, Los Angeles, California
Mrs. Mary Riepma Ross, New York
Mr. and Mrs. Louis Sosland, Shawnee Mission,
 Kansas
Mr. Milfred Tokoph, Highland Park, Illinois
Mr. Chauncey L. Waddell, New York
Mr. and Mrs. Hudson Walker, Forest Hills, New York

Allan Frumkin Gallery, Chicago, Illinois
Allan Frumkin Gallery, New York
Babcock Galleries, New York
Egan Gallery, New York
Felix Landau Gallery, Los Angeles, California
Galerie Claude Bernard, Paris, France

Gilman Gallery, Chicago, Illinois
Graham Gallery Ltd., New York
Poindexter Gallery, New York
Tibor de Nagy Gallery, New York

Albright-Knox Art Gallery, Buffalo, New York
Andrew Dickson White Museum of Art,
 Cornell University, Ithaca, New York
Bowdoin College Museum of Art, Brunswick,
 Maine
Commerce Trust Company, Kansas City, Missouri
Goodall Gallery, Doane College, Crete, Nebraska
Indiana University Fine Arts Museum,
 Bloomington, Indiana
Metropolitan Museum of Art, New York
Museo de Bellas Artes, Caracas, Venezuela
Museum of Fine Arts, Springfield, Massachusetts
Museum of Modern Art, New York
National Academy of Design, New York
Nebraska Art Association, Lincoln, Nebraska
Sara Roby Foundation, New York
University of Nebraska Art Galleries, Lincoln,
 Nebraska
Whitney Museum of American Art, New York

In accepting the invitation of the National Collection of Fine Arts, Smithsonian Institution, to organize the American exhibition at the XXXIV Biennale at Venice we are particularly aware, not only of the honor and obligation involved, but also of the place of this exhibition in a long sequence of exhibitions, the relationship of the exhibition to the American art scene as a whole, and of the expectations of the foreign audience, both lay and professional, who will visit the Biennale. That the National Collection of Fine Arts has chosen our proposals for the exhibition is a gesture of confidence which we acknowledge with appreciation.

On behalf of the University of Nebraska, I would like to express special appreciation to the staff of the International Art Program, National Collection of Fine Arts for the help and counsel which have made the task much less taxing than it would have been otherwise. To have worked with David W. Scott and Lois Bingham on this project has been a pleasure throughout. The experience has provided a lasting demonstration of the reality of a responsible concern for the public as well as professional interests involved.

The physical production of the catalog and exhibition were facilitated in innumerable ways by the experience and skill of Margaret Cogswell, Deputy Chief of the International Art Program. The translation, no mean task in itself, is the work of Giordano Falzoni.

Charles Forberg Associates, New York, have designed the exhibit installation with taste and skill. Bert Clarke, of Clarke and Way, has been an unfailing source of advice in the design and production of the catalog.

The staff of the University Art Galleries has contributed in many ways to the successful realization of the exhibition and the catalog. My special thanks to Jon Nelson, who, with the assistance of Edith Renne, assembled the biographical and bibliographical data. The design for the catalog is the work of Dwight Stark.

The biographical note and selected bibliography pertaining to Reuben Nakian are the work of Miss Cynthia Jaffe who is assembling the definitive information on this artist.

We have a special indebtedness to the List Art Poster Program for the enhancement provided by the poster, commissioned from Carol Summers, which will accompany the exhibition both in Italy and at home.

Lastly and most importantly, we are indebted to the artists, their dealers, the museums and private collectors who supported our many requests for information and confirmation. Their generosity in permitting us to use the selected works for more than a year is of the utmost importance to the entire project.

Norman A. Geske
Director, University of Nebraska Art Galleries

Table of Contents

Foreword

(letter to the Editor, *Art International*, June, 1968, from Norman A. Geske)

Selecting the American exhibition for the 34th Biennale is a tonic experience. One learns very quickly the truth of the adage having to do with pleasing people, if that by chance has not been any part of one's operational credo up to the moment. One also learns that the forces of fashion and publicity are far stronger than one had supposed. In any case, to be pushed into the spotlight on an international stage is an unsettling experience and tonic only if one's convictions can be mustered in sufficient strength to get one's back up.

Last summer when the invitation to consider selecting the American show at Venice was received I sat down with myself to consider what I might do if the choice really became mine. Thinking back on the Biennales of 1966, and 1962 and 1960 (I missed the epochal show of 1964—but who could miss its impact?) it seemed very simple. All the signs were clearly writ. Abstract Expressionism and Pop and Op and Post-painterly abstraction had all been given their due, in turn. These were handsome, lively, challenging exhibitions which demonstrated that the United States was indeed out in front. The occasion to come was as predictable as sunrise—1968 should be the year for a judicious mixture of Minimal and Funk. On the one hand there would be a choice among Tony Smith, Donald Judd, Ronald Bladen, James McCracken, Robert Morris, Robert Grosvenor or a half dozen more possibilities, or, if light is the kick, Stephen Antonakos, Chryssa, or Dan Flavin, or, if it is color in movement or suspension, then there would be Larry Bell or Fletcher Benton or Norman Zammitt. With these strict, and disciplined, and rejective types it would be nice for contrast to have some of the latter-day expressionists like Edward Kienholz or Bruce Conner, or some of the fantasists of Funk, Robert Hudson or Kenneth Price or Peter Saul, with maybe the leaven of some of the relative conservatism of John Chamberlain or Mark Di Suvero.

With very little time given to the problem, I had a show. And then a sensation of sheer stubborn contrariness overcame me and I thought that I'd rather not be caught in quite so neat a situation. Why should the Smithsonian or any other responsible agency pick me or anyone else to spend a lot of time and money on what could obviously be done more simply and cheaply by a rapid run through of the "ten best one-man shows of 1967."

It was not altogether easy to resist so clearly marked a path. This would be—if not easy—at least an easier way to acquire a Conner, a Tony Smith and a Di Suvero, all of whom I would very much like to have represented in the art collection for which I am primarily responsible.

Anyway, it suddenly seemed to me that if the situation was that simple and obvious there must be an alternative, less simple and less obvious, but of equal merit. And I recalled a notion that has been bugging me for the last few years, that there was something afoot among the practitioners of figurative art. Admittedly, a little of the thunder of this notion had already been stolen by the masters of Pop, some of whom have already been shown at Venice, but it wasn't the Pop artists who were crowding me. Instead, it was a sizeable group of painters and sculptors, some of whom were old enough to have lived through the diversionary decades of the New York School and what came after. Some were born into the middle of it, had to decide somewhere along the way that total abstraction was not for them, and had to start over, and late, to be themselves. Others were, and are, too young to have ever been concerned, except unconsciously. There are quite a few of these artists: a remarkable older generation dominated by Hopper and Avery and Dickinson, and among the "younger" men one could choose from Fairfield Porter, Byron Burford, Hiram Williams, Philip Pearlstein, Paul Georges, Richard Diebenkorn, Elmer Bischoff, James Gill, John Paul Jones, Wayne Thiebaud, Leon Golub.

Among the sculptors it is harder, but there is some mighty impressive figuration in the work of George Segal, Ernest Trova, Leonard Baskin, Robert Cremean, Frank Gallo; and we have a master in Reuben Nakian.

All these possibilities added up to a challenging conclusion. Whatever it is that is afoot in recent figuration might be worth looking at in a context such as that provided at Venice and worth pointing out to others. It might be possible to say, "Look, the maturity of American art is not the exclusive attribute of Pollock, Rothko and Kline, nor, indeed, even of any one of the developments since. It is a pervasive thing and nowhere is it any clearer than in the middle of our tradition, close to the root."

The Smithsonian seemed to get the idea as I described it. They have a good idea concerning these shows and I hope they hold to it (although saying so here and now certainly smacks of self-justification). They propose to ask concerned and qualified directors and curators from all parts of the country to organize these international shows. These will be different people from different kinds of institutions, who, hopefully do not all subscribe to the same magazines or patronize the same dealers. Thus, it may be that the international audience, which ostensibly justifies Venice and São Paulo, will see a broader range of American talent, and receive a more varied impression of the American art scene as a whole.

If, as some of the more cynical members of our art establishment maintain, the Biennale is only a commercial showcase for the so-called avant garde, then the American Pavilion in 1968 is going to be "something else."

In the present exhibition the intention has been to demonstrate the continuing vitality of the figurative tradition in recent American art. After somewhat more than twenty years, during which American artists achieved international leadership by demonstrating the possibility and the vitality of a completely abstract mode of seeing, it is now perfectly clear that figuration is once again a serious vehicle of expression for many American artists. All through this period, of course, some asserted the point of view that nature is still concentrated in its most revealing form in the body of man and in his environment. While it is demonstrable that this tradition never ceased to have its practitioners, even during the ascendancy of abstract expressionism, it is equally demonstrable that the present practice of figuration is quite different from that of the earlier decades of the present century, and that its present strength is due in large part to the experience of abstraction itself in the more recent past.

To assess the importance of American Abstract Expressionism with reference to the development of figurative art is not simple, but it is essential. Perhaps it can be said, at least, that the movement served to purge the American artistic conscience of every shred of its inherited sense of obligation to the traditional ideal of communication. As a national experience it had the effect of a gigantic demolition which removed not only the whole inherited structure of American provincialism, but established for the first time an American disinterest in any source of inspiration other than its own capabilities. For the first time American painters did not care what their relationship to London, Paris, Rome or Düsseldorf might be. The clearing away of these psychological ties had an effect which will not be calculable for a long time, but it is clear enough that nothing in our artistic life has been quite the same since.

If we look briefly at this event of some twenty years duration, we can see that the most important talents of the period were engaged in a struggle with none other than our immediate subject, the figure. In the work of Arshile Gorky from the decade 1926–1936, and that of Jackson Pollock from the early nineteen-forties, we can see the figure literally fading away in the headlong impulse to achieve the purity of total abstraction. In the work of Philip Guston, there is almost a note of wrenching agony in the dark, tormented impastos of the pictures of 1947–48 which mark his break with a successful career as a figurative artist. It is important to remember Pollock's recall of figurative ideas in the pictures of 1950–51 and Willem DeKooning's intermittent preoccupation with the figure which, only of late, has resolved itself in an almost obsessive sublimation of the figure.

The other, more philosophical, aspect of the school, expressed in the work of Still, Rothko, and Newman, maintained its freedom from obvious figural concerns. However, one has only to read some of the statements made by these men to realize that while they may not be concerned with specific figuration, they are deeply concerned with a humanistic rationalization of experience.

Abstract Expressionism, for all its superficial sameness, has demonstrated with astounding variety the range of individual response to experience. There is in Marca-Relli a magisterial organization, in James Brooks a superb athleticism, in Okada a palpable serenity, in Ad Reinhardt the dryness of thought itself; in the work of Joan Mitchell, Esteban Vicente, Jack Tworkov, Hassel Smith, Grace Hartigan, and perhaps a dozen more, there is a non-figurative art which has established a fresh view of the world, and which has been taken up, exploited and developed in a variety of new directions.

Possibly the most significant of these directions has been that initiated in the work of Robert Rauschenberg, Jasper Johns, and Jim Dine. After the spatial solemnity of the vast canvases, the autographic ritual of gesture, and the veils or thunderheads of color, the sudden audacity of applying these very elements to figuration of the most obvious kind was stimulation enough to raise the question of subject matter once again. Restored to life in the naive simplicity of such forms as American flags, targets, and calendars, chickens, goats, and tennis shoes, the subject returned in triumph disguised as object. These artists established the bridgehead through which the development of a renewed figurative art could flow unimpeded. The ultra subjectivity of Abstract Expressionism had its answer in the commonplace symbology of Pop. Within this entire development there is a kidding good humor that sometimes takes on the derisive character of a jeer. There is also a good deal of purely commercial sophistication, a tongue-in-cheek acceptance of face values, and an enormous facility in technical matters that attains an appropriate kind of super-elegance. The figuration encountered in Claes Oldenburg, Tom Wesselmann, or Roy Lichtenstein is indeed of an order that is new not only in scale but in its celebration of vulgarities of an unprecedented variety. This elevation of the subject matter of Everyman to the level of universal symbol has in fact reached an almost fetishistic concern with the lowest common denominators of visual experience. It might be said that, in effect, the vulgarity of Pop has been mathematically squared by Funk.

This newest offshoot is substantially Dadaist in its defiance of the proprieties. At their most polite the works of Funk are merely mischievous, audacious, rude, and raucous, but the guts of the matter are to be found in a high degree of erotic suggestivity which at moments qualifies in every sense of the word as visual scatology. As in every movement, there are individuals who have exploited the ideas involved for the sake of publicity. However, there are also a few artists of serious intention who are usually the originators of a style long before it is given a name and who are eventually swallowed up in the crowd of their imitators. In this instance two artists of genuine insight and technical originality must be acknowledged. They are Bruce Conner and Edward Kienholz, both creators of an ugliness that approaches the sublime. Both create works which affront the viewer to a degree that has on occasion prevented them from reaching the public, but the penetration of their comment on contemporary experience is such that their work, once seen, is unforgettable.

If both Pop and Funk may be credited in their origins to a direct descent from Abstract Expressionism, there are still other tendencies which relate to it in different ways, some by way of a refinement of elements, some by way of reaction, some by way of underground survival. The first of such tendencies can be traced to the intuitive color research of the kind found in the paintings of Mark Rothko. This demonstration of the power of color has found an ally in the concepts of geometric painting, which until recently have never enjoyed a wide practice or a receptive audience in the United States. The play of pure color can be pure calisthenics for the eye, or applied to landscape or the figure it can evoke an ambiance of undeniable particularity and power; witness the landscapes of Allan D'Arcangelo or Edward Ruscha and the figure compositions of James Strombotne or Byron Burford. In the work of Burford there has always been a concern with the evocative power of color. He has not only tested it to the full in figure and landscape themes, but has explored its use in themes of much more complex character with unusual success. There are also artists who have emerged from an apprenticeship in abstraction to embrace a concept of painting that is closer to Corot than to Cézanne. All hint of Expressionist crisis or of the dynamics of reform is missing. There is an ease in the way which the pictures coalesce as images, a confidence in the simple exercise of the eye, a response that makes no demand on theory or fashion. Frequently and unabashedly there is the clear echo of historic precedent. It is usually a pre-revolutionary, that is, a pre-Impressionist echo of Corot or Barbizon, or of such remote schools as Flemish and Italian Renaissance portraiture, or even British or early American Romanticism. For these painters the subjects are again of the simple unequivocal kind, objects arranged on a table, the model in the studio, a panorama of unremarkable landscape, but they are handled with a purity of interest and a directness of touch that owe much to the Abstract Expressionist ideal of a painterly art. Among the artists who represent this attitude, some of whom have been pupils of Hans Hofmann, the patriarch of Abstract Expressionism, are Leland Bell, Robert DeNiro, Jane Wilson, Jane Freilicher, Paul Georges, Seymour Remenick, George Deem, and Paul Resika. This aspect of present-day figuration is represented here by one of the most intuitively accomplished of them all, Fairfield Porter. In his work this kind of uncomplicated vision is combined with knowledge and skill in a blend that sums up to perfection the simple but essential idea of the painter as picture maker.

Next in our consideration are those figurative painters who might be said to have survived the period of abstraction without having been in any real sense a part of it. They are the artistic individualists who at an early stage in their careers found the manner of working which for them produced the most satisfying result. They have frequently paid for such independence with decades of neglect, but with the passing of the revolution of abstraction and the discovery by younger men that the abstract solutions were not necessarily ultimate, these artists have come back into public attention. Such artists are Milton Avery, Edward Hopper, and in the present exhibition, Edwin Dickinson. Their prescience was and is remarkable. Avery's color in all its luminous peculiarity and the magical balance of his composition; Hopper's rigor, his bitter color, his total lack of ingratiation; and, lastly, the inventive power and innate feeling for the rendering of form which is the distinction of Edwin Dickinson, are all visible elements in the work of younger men and vivid evidence of the persistent strength of tradition.

Certain other artists have derived their principal inspirations from the Expressionism and Surrealism of the post-war years. This latter-day Expressionism lacks the emotional heat of the historic prototypes. Primitivism and psychosis are replaced by a candid fantasy, a thoroughly objective self-indulgence in imaginative and psychological possibilities. Robert Beauchamp is perhaps the most typical exponent of this kind of painting and Lester Johnson is similarly skilled at making an immediate impression with the scale and impetuosity of his works.

Other expressionists concern themselves with a more externalized observation of society. Two of the best are Hiram Williams and James Gill, both critics in the historic sense, providing depictions of contemporary urban man which have the bite of truth, images of ourselves distorted by the processes of self-delusion as well as by the peculiarly cinematographic quality of their vision.

A more complicated artist, richer in the variety of his sources, more challengingly allusive in his imagery, altogether more virtuoso in the range of his technique, is James McGarrell. He achieves something rare in American painting, an imagery with many levels of meaning, visual, literary, and psychological. His expressionism is perhaps the subtlest of any among his contemporaries, and also the most openly inventive.

In California, in the hands of half a dozen gifted painters, there has developed the single regional school of any consequence in the past decade. The group includes David Park, who died at the age of forty-nine in 1960, Elmer Bischoff, Richard Diebenkorn, James Weeks, Paul Wonner, and William Theo Brown. Closely related to them are some younger painters, Nathan Oliveira, Joan Brown, and Roland Peterson. Related at its root to the expressionist idea of art and brought to fruition through the processes of Abstract Expressionism, this school has developed a community of vision and a technique which is very like that which existed among the Impressionists. It is a style which is somewhat academic in subject, or at least unexceptional; its main characteristic is found in its materiality, in the rich, oily flow of pigment, sometimes in broad washes, sometimes in dense manipulations within a fairly rigid patterning of the canvas. At the beginning of their careers the work of all of these men was in a wholly abstract style. Subsequently they returned to figuration and created a refulgent Californian kind of picture, dominated by a strong sense of the out-of-doors, of the hot sun and a blare of tropical color. Their most characteristic image is the classic one of bathers in a landscape, which affords them the perfect vehicle for their essentially hedonistic point of view. Richard Diebenkorn is possibly the most impressive of the group by virtue of his rather greater sense of discipline in composition and the relationship of color, which results in a very personal kind of tautness. His pictures reverberate with the combined resonance of light and color. Although not related in any circumstantial way to this group, Wayne Thiebaud is interested in much the same kind of emphatic, brilliantly colored picture making. Often included among the masters of Pop, he is actually a much more conventional artist. His commitment to a mundane range of subjects has in it an appreciative warmth rather than anything of the cynical or clever.

The one last aspect of recent figuration which merits our attention is that usually described as realistic. This is a way of seeing which has always enjoyed special favor with Americans, including as it does some of our greatest painters from Copley to Eakins. In the present century, aside from those painters of the social scene who flourished during the thirties, there have not been many realists of quality. Of course, one can cite that species of realism which seems to exist in a sub-strata of its own at practically all periods, which in the nineteen-forties and fifties was commonly described as Magic Realism. There are still painters in this style everywhere and their work is frequently qualified for the attention of the observer only by some degree of erotic or surrealist overtone.

There is, however, a stronger vein of realism in the work of a group of painters who cannot properly be considered with those of the illusionist or surrealist persuasion just mentioned. Certainly the finest painter of this style and unquestionably the most popular artist in the United States is Andrew Wyeth. He is no surrealist. His distinction is a completely intelligent eye, a remarkable balance of physical, intellectual, and emotional impulses. He has a host of imitators who can be detected in the majority of instances by a total lack of air in their pictures.

Of more interest to a narrower public is the extraordinary painting of Philip Pearlstein. Here is an artist whose interests have never excluded the direct observation of natural form, although at one point, some ten years or more ago, his pictures were clearly dominated by the gestural rhythm of Expressionism. Moving from an exhaustive preoccupation with landscape, seen close-up, he has undertaken an equally exhaustive analysis of the nude which he treats much like the landscape, as a purely formal phenomenon. These paintings are superb objectifications of experienced form. They are probably the most non-sensuous nudes in contemporary art, realized with the kind of intellectual vigor that recalls Thomas Eakins. Pearlstein's is a remarkable achievement in a period of ultimate permissiveness.

This same kind of factual vision is also seen in the work of Malcolm Morley and Lowell Nesbitt. Morley's is a peculiar kind of reseeing, which accepts the total, complete image, as given in a completely ordinary commercial context, usually some kind of full-color advertisement, and recreates it in an act of visual sleight of hand. First contact with Morley's paintings is a purely *trompe l'oeil* experience until one realizes that the artist's choice of image and his immersion in it, is, in a sense, identical with that of the observer and that it is the recognition of this fact which is the gist of the matter, surely the subtlest of achievements. Lowell Nesbitt works in much the same way, except that his personal view is discernible to a much more noticeable degree. Both artists represent an acceptive kind of vision quite different from the concentrated banality of much Pop art. This is an acceptance that is perhaps best described by that old, almost forgotten term, classical.

The story of American sculptural developments is not essentially different from that of painting, except for the fact that it has only been in the present century that the United States has produced anything like a major sculptural talent. Consideration as such can surely be accorded Elie Nadelman, William Zorach, Gaston Lachaise, Alexander Calder, and David Smith. It is in the work of these five men that the stages of our sculptural history in this century can be charted. They are the major forerunners of the men whose work is shown in the present exhibition.

Nadelman and Lachaise, both foreign born and bringing with them to the United States an inheritance of European tradition, sum up with striking singularity the exact character of a transitional art. There is a marked technical facility in their work which creates forms of extraordinary finish and refinement, embodying all the mingled classic and romantic elements which represent nineteenth-century sculptural thinking at its most erudite level. It is significant, however, that both Nadelman and Lachaise were artists of immense potential and their development was a continuous thing, refining inherited strengths and testing these against the demands of ever more daring concepts until the very end of their respective careers. There is in the work of both men a considerable element of forecast as well as a summing-up. It can be said of William Zorach that he was the classical example of artistic talent born of a European background but developed in the circumstances of the American environment. First of all a painter, he developed his sculptural style out of deeply personal resources. He was perhaps the finest representative of the whole school of American sculptors who established the concept of direct carving in a simplified, somewhat classicizing style as the dominant sculptural method for several decades. Other notable representatives of direct carving are Oronzio Maldarelli, Robert Laurent, and José de Creeft, all of whom contributed substantially to the level of craftsmanship which characterized the group. An exception was John B. Flannagan, whose primitivistic simplicity set him apart in the world of his own mystical imagination.

During the period of the nineteen-thirties when painting and the graphic arts were devoted to regionalism and satirical realism, sculpture was in no way exceptional. It is noteworthy that in such a situation, which did not favor or encourage formal experimentation, there developed two of the authentic masters of American sculptural art, Alexander Calder and David Smith.

Calder, the son of a famous academician, began his career with satiric or witty works made of wire, significantly free of concern with the traditional elements of sculpture such as mass and volume in the conventional sense. He did not visit Paris until well after World War I, but once there he became the friend and associate of all the leaders of French art, and he has maintained his connections with France to the present. Calder is the kind of artist who can assimilate for his own use any innovation created by another artist, yet even with the occasional suggestion of influence from Van Doesburg or Arp or Miró, there is an overriding personality which is Calder. His two inventions, the mobile and the stabile, so named by Duchamp and Arp respectively, are among the very few truly original artistic ideas of our time. His universe of flickering, gliding, undulant forms which exist only as patterns of movement in space is entirely his own. Surely space, that obsessive artistic preoccupation of the present century, has rarely if ever had so eloquent an embodiment. The rise within the present decade of an American enthusiasm for kinetic art is in large part due to the example of Alexander Calder. It is also notable that with all the many post-Calder variations that have come into being, Calder's own gifts, his wit, lyricism, and sheer audacity, are as clear, unmistakable, and inimitable as ever.

Of David Smith there is much more to be said, for he is not the unique phenomenon that is Calder. Smith is one of a whole generation of American sculptors who took up and developed the techniques of industrial fabrication on a scale that gave American sculpture, for the first time, the heady stimulation of creative leadership. Sharing this leadership with Smith are such others as David Hare, Ibram Lassaw, Theodore Roszak, Herbert Ferber, and Seymour Lipton. These men have developed highly personal styles, and together they have given sculptural practice an entirely new vocabulary, making possible the expression of a whole range of new subject matter: symbolic, psychological, and purely abstract in the sense of a totally open suggestivity. In a very real sense, this was an accomplishment of the utmost peculiarity to our times.

To set David Smith apart is justifiable on several counts. Following the lead of Picasso and Gonzalez, he was probably the first American artist to work with scrap material in a welded format. His work during a period of more than thirty years shows a greater variety of ideas than is seen in the work of any of the others. His sense of space and scale and texture and color is stronger, bolder, more demanding, and more revealing. Smith seems to include more of life than anyone else in his generation. His influence, since his tragic death in 1965, continues to affect the art of sculpture in a variety of ways.

In addition to these five, there are few other choices among our contemporaries, the strongest possibilities being Isamu Noguchi and Louise Nevelson. Noguchi is, in a way, similar to Nadelman and Lachaise, a continuator of traditions, this time a blend of Europe and the Orient. His essential statement is, however, his own and not dependent on these sources. It is an allusive, poetic kind of sculpture varying from the austere and mysterious to the witty and elegant; it is an art which is supremely civilized, learned, cosmopolitan. His is the only hand today that works stone, metal, wood, and clay with such equal ease and versatility.

Nevelson is a narrower artist but deeper. Her talent has achieved its real flowering late, but she has more than made up for this by the flow of her invention since the early nineteen-fifties. Creator of boxes, walls, altars, and veritable landscapes, she has the power to speak in the simplest terms, of black and white and gold, of darkness and light. Among all the important sculptors of the day, hers is the most extraordinary gift for transformation, wherein painted wood achieves an evocative power that has not been surpassed in her more recent work in more elegant materials. She is the priestess of mystery, the mistress of an incantatory visual style.

Among these possibilities there is one more, Reuben Nakian. He, like Nevelson, is a late blooming talent. Like Noguchi, he is a poet of the sensuous. Like Smith, he can muster a superbly masculine candor. Like Calder, he stands quite by himself in the individuality of his technique. Unlike them all, he has chosen to remain close to the idea of figuration and in this sense his achievement is the more remarkable, for the simple reason that it encompasses the experience of abstract expressionism without severing the final link with anthropomorphic form. It bears the impact of a spatial concept of form as a continuum and demonstrates the processes of sculpture, the building, welding, draping, cutting, casting, coloring, modeling as a gestural vocabulary capable of registering the subjective immediacy of emotional impulse in a way rarely seen in earlier practice.

Nakian's relationship to the problems of figuration in recent sculpture is important, although his work is really bigger in its grasp and more intensely felt in its mood than much of the work of younger men. At the moment, the situation is full of ideas originating in geometric abstraction, Dada, Pop, Op, and Funk. None of these sources of inspiration imply an art of his kind. For example, the great final outburst of David Smith's career, which produced the magnificent series of Cubi, contributed in an important way to an outpouring of very large sculptures, built of industrial steel and colored with the blinding hues of industrial finish. This is a sculpture which presages a new concept of its function, as a partner rather than an ornament to architecture, and as a major participant in urban design and total landscape. Another Smith, Tony Smith, has emerged from a long career of relative obscurity as a painter and architect as the most commanding of these artists. His work is very like that of David Smith in the clean boldness of its scale, and, in a way, like Nevelson in its suggestive range, but it is unmistakably the work of Tony Smith. The evocative power of his geometry is quite unlike anything we have achieved to date.

Of a totally different kind is the clinical realism of a number of artists, whose concern with environment and involvement has produced works which may be considered as sculpture or, just as frequently, as paintings. We have already discussed this development in the work of Edward Kienholz and Bruce Conner. Among the viable alternatives to either of these directions is a more traditional figuration which, though less adventurous, less emphatic, less passionate, or, as the case may be, less cool in its commitments, is nevertheless undergoing a notable revival in the hands of a few gifted artists. Admittedly, the number of these artists is small, far smaller than the number carried by the band wagons of the more fashionable styles. Admittedly, they are either holdouts from the Abstract Expressionist fashion or they have appeared on the scene so recently that they are still immune to its point of view. In any case, they are present and they are asserting themselves in a way which commands our attention and our interest.

Hewing to the very center of traditional practices of carving, modeling, and casting are such artists as Leonard Baskin, Paul Granlund, and Richard Miller. Of these Baskin is the most distinctive, mainly by reason of the deeply personal cast which his work possesses, but also because of the deliberate and persistent way in which he calls upon history in the continuing flow of his work. The great men, works, and ideas of the past are invoked with all the persuasive emotion he commands to establish an artistic position *vis à vis* the present. There is more than a touch of the prophet's thunder about Baskin, but his convictions are founded on a scholar's knowledge, and his work remains unassailably right in the plastic integrity of its statement. Paul Granlund, on the other hand, seeks his inspiration in masters who have never figured in Baskin's pantheon, in Rodin and Degas, and justifies his choice in his exploration of the iconography of the human body, finding fresh possibilities that seem to extend these masters into our own time. There is about his figures a familiar mood of *angst*. They are containers of doubt, spiritually as well as literally tied in knots, twisting and turning in relationships which are governed by anxiety or, sometimes, ecstasy. Richard Miller, of the three, is the purist, fascinated by the female form in a way that has not seemed relevant for a long time, but which now appears peculiarly right again in the "coolness" of his concern, wherein sensuosity and psychology are subordinated to a candid naturalism.

There are also figurative sculptors who move farther away from the central stream of Realism, into more specifically personal interpretations. Noteworthy among them is Robert Cremean, whose work is virtuoso in technique and challengingly ambiguous in meaning. One rarely knows for certain what the specific meaning of Cremean's statement may be; it is always subject to contending interpretations of surprisingly equal strength. There is at times a choreographic variety of movement that suggests only a simple pleasure in plastic elegance, but at other times there is the strong suggestion of a troubled spirit, of attitudes and concerns of a shadowed and introspective kind. A rather special case is the work of Ernest Trova. While it exemplifies the perfection of mass-production methods often seen in the work of sculptors inspired by constructivist theories, it is also haunted by that troubled self-concern which only asks questions and does not presume to suggest answers.

The overt and often exuberant emotionalism of Expressionism is found at full force in the work of such artists as Jack Zajac and Elbert Weinberg, both of whom have felt the impact of religious themes. Zajac's most recent work, consisting of solitary and monu-mentalized fragments, marks a promising development in his style toward a simpler and more direct symbolism. A more cerebral kind of expressionism is found in the work of Harold Tovish, who formerly cultivated the ideal of primitivism but who now concentrates on highly finished forms that lend themselves to a disturbing sculptural illusionism.

There are few notable exponents of the kind of sculpture which comments on its subject in terms of satire. The most effective are William King and, more recently, Frank Gallo. King's wit is sly and gentle. His viewpoint is always amused, never critical. His most recent ventures into works executed in synthetic fabrics, stuffed and propped like gargantuan—or miniature—puppets, are perhaps his most detached works to date, if one can assess the warmth of their motivating impulse.

Frank Gallo's epoxy resin figures are a notable technical achievement quite apart from their possible meaning, but it is in their evaluation of a sensuous society that their interest lies. Aside from their unselfconscious eroticism, there is also a subtle penetration of mood, again a mood of anxiety, which perhaps suggests their essential meaning.

We have already referred to the presence of Pop in the mixture of influences which are currently in evidence. It would not be accurate or fair to overlook the sculptors most often identified with this style who are, in every sense of the word, students of figuration. If we consider them even briefly, it can be seen that their work appears to be surviving the curse of the name. The artists in question are George Segal, Marisol, Claes Olden-burg, and Red Grooms. All four are primarily concerned with a personal view of man, his artifacts, and his environment. All four would seem to be in dead earnest, and all four can and do impel an after-effect of thought and recognition which is as good as any test of their seriousness. Segal's plaster images, frozen in the ambiance of commonplace reality, are indelible. Marisol's carpentered images are miracles of witty, frequently stinging, observation. In some of her work, for instance in her tandem *Washington and Bolivar* on hobby-horseback (in the collection of the Albright-Knox Art Gallery) and in her most recent series called *Heads of State*, she has demonstrated a satiric gift of uncommon originality. In Oldenburg's soft blow-up of an ashtray full of cigarette butts, or a jazz musician's set of drums, or a paper bag full of French fries, we encounter with sobering impact the dominating trivia of contemporary life, and yet it may be that Oldenburg would not have us see them otherwise. Last of this group, Red Grooms is the most natural, the most up-beat and, in some ways, the most traditionally American. The innate simplicity of his make-believe, which approaches the problem at ground level, has at this point the impact of revelation.

The figurative painting and sculpture being produced by American artists today is quite distinct from that which was current before the ascendancy of Abstract Expressionism. It is, first of all, different in its formal means, being freer, more intuitively inventive than before. It is also different in its point of view, seeing its subject with a purely visual kind of objectivity. The obsolescent aspects of historic figuration have been eliminated and it is a different image which confronts us today. In the work of many American artists this renewal is clear and full of promise.

Norman A. Geske

There is probably no living American artist of consequence with so comprehensive a relationship to the art of the past, who, at the same time, is able to assert a contemporary point of view of such pertinence and power. The roster of his spiritual ancestors, to whom he continues to make obeisance, is a long one: Barlach, Blake, Brecht, Bresdin, Callot, Eakins, Mahler, Mantegna, Redon, Rembrandt, to name only those who come to mind at once. His is an erudition of astounding proportions, but it is not simply that, for his interest in the past is impelled by his insatiable hunger for a confirmation of the present. It is doubtful that Baskin thinks of man as progressive. For him the human potential is a constant thing, constantly fed and illuminated by the understanding of artists. His own understanding is fed and confirmed by the example of artists before him.

There is no doubt that Baskin is a whole-hearted champion of human causes, and it has only been by virtue of his commanding skill that his arguments on behalf of man and society have had any currency during a period which has made a cult of disengagement. His admiration for artists such as Barlach and Callot is evidenced not merely in plastic terms, but in terms of his commitment to the role of artist as observer, commentator, and prophet.

In the strictest sense his most important achievement has been in the realm of graphic art, in an astounding series of woodcuts, wood engravings, etchings, lithographs, drawings, and illustrated books. Few, if any, American graphic artists of our day have Baskin's natural genius for statement in black and white. The simplicity of his graphics, which is achieved at times through an almost fiendish virtuosity, is matched with a sense of scale and an impassioned immediacy of feeling which is all but unique. Surely unique at present is his creation of the Gehenna Press, which has published a long series of meticulously produced books of the highest quality. These elegant volumes contain not only texts of his own choosing but illustrations, papers, type faces, and bindings which provide a distinct aesthetic pleasure to the eye and the hand.

However gifted as a graphic artist, Baskin must be taken seriously as a sculptor. Here his most personal achievements are a series of wood carvings, both large and small. This material has had only a meagre popularity in recent years, chiefly among sculptors who work in the manner of abstract assemblage. Baskin's standing and seated figures have been wholly exceptional and certainly his affinity with Ernst Barlach is very clear. These carvings have achieved not only an extraordinary mastery of medium and technique, but an amazing interpretive quality as well, an almost sentient elasticity of form which makes the figures fairly breathe in the light surrounding them.

In bronze Baskin's distinctive touch is seen in the initial modeling of the forms which, when cast and finished with his favorite black patina, reflect the light with a kind of pitiless sobriety. His *Achilles Mourning the Death of Patrocles* has about it an impression of inert weight, filled with the blunt shock of grief. This is expressed as much in the simplification of the forms and the insistent play of light over them, as it is in the maimed helplessness of the figure itself.

Leonard Baskin has been for more than ten years the potent counterpoise to the almost universal prevalence of abstraction in American art. He has been outspoken in his concern and has assumed all the risks of a dedicated polemicist, but his example, which at times has appeared to be solitary, has been an unshakeable link with the tradition of figuration.

Biographical Note

Born, New Brunswick, New Jersey, 1922

Education
1937–1939, special studies with Maurice Glickman; 1939–1941, New York University School of Architecture and Allied Arts, New York; 1941–1943, Yale University School of Fine Arts; 1949, The New School for Social Research; 1950, Académie de la Grande Chaumière, Paris, France; 1951, Academy of Fine Arts, Florence, Italy

Teaching Positions
1953, Instructor in printmaking, Worcester Art Museum, Worcester, Massachusetts; 1953 to present, Professor in drawing, printmaking, and sculpture, Smith College, Northampton, Massachusetts

One-man Exhibitions
1939, Glickman Studio Gallery, New York; 1940, Gallery of the New York University School of Architecture and Allied Arts, New York; 1951, Gallery "Numero," Florence, Italy; 1952, The Little Gallery, Princeton, New Jersey; 1952, Mount Holyoke College, South Hadley, Massachusetts; 1953, Fitchburg Art Museum, Fitchburg, Massachusetts; 1953, 1955, 1956, 1957, 1958, 1960, 1962, 1964, 1966, Grace Borgenicht Gallery, New York; 1952, 1953, 1957, 1959, 1960, 1962, 1964, 1965, 1967, Boris Mirski Gallery, Boston, Massachusetts; 1957, Worcester Art Museum, Worcester, Massachusetts; 1959, University of California, Berkeley, California; 1959, Philadelphia Print Club, Philadelphia, Pennsylvania; 1959, Pasadena Art Museum, Pasadena, California; 1961, Boymans Museum, Rotterdam, Netherlands; 1961, Amerika Haus, Berlin, Germany; 1961, Le Centre Culturel Americain, Paris, France; 1962, The Royal

Watercolor Society with St. George's Gallery, London, England; 1962, Bowdoin College Museum of Art, Brunswick, Maine; 1966, Peale House, Pennsylvania Academy of the Fine Arts, Philadelphia, Pennsylvania

Honors and Awards
1940, Prix de Rome, Honorable Mention for Sculpture; 1941, Scholarship to Yale University School of Fine Art; 1947, Louis Comfort Tiffany Foundation Fellowship for Sculpture; 1952, Print Club of Philadelphia, 26th Annual Exhibition of Prints, Purchase Prize; 1953, Brooklyn Museum 7th Annual of Prints, Purchase Prize; 1953, Guggenheim Fellowship in Creative Printmaking; 1953, Wylon, International Society of Wood Engravers, Zurich, Switzerland; 1954, O'Hara Museum Prize, Japanese National Museum of Tokyo; 1961, Alonzo C. Mather Prize, Chicago Art Institute; 1961, São Paulo Bienal, Best Foreign Engraver; 1965, American Institute of Graphic Art, Special Medal of Merit; 1965, Pennsylvania Academy of the Fine Arts, Widener Medal

Public Collections
Academy of Natural Science, Philadelphia, Pennsylvania; Albion College, Albion, Ohio; Alverthorpe Gallery, Jenkintown, Pennsylvania; Albright-Knox Art Gallery, Buffalo, New York; Allegheny College, Meadville, Pennsylvania; Art Institute of Chicago, Chicago, Illinois; Bezalel National Museum, Jerusalem; Brandeis University, Waltham, Massachusetts; Brooklyn Museum, Brooklyn, New York; Chase Manhattan Bank, New York; City Art Museum of St. Louis, St. Louis, Missouri; Wesleyan University, Middletown, Connecticut; Detroit Institute of Arts, Detroit, Michigan; Fitchburg Museum, Fitchburg, Massachusetts; Harvard University, Cambridge, Massachusetts; Holyoke Public Library, Holyoke, Massachusetts; University of Illinois, Champaign-Urbana, Illinois; Kunst Pä Arbeidsplassen, Oslo, Norway; Library of Congress, Washington, D.C.; Marshall College, Huntington, West Virginia; Mt. Holyoke College, South Hadley, Massachusetts; Munson-Williams-Proctor Institute, Utica, New York; Museum of Modern Art, New York; Museum of Fine Arts, Boston, Massachusetts; National Gallery of Art, Washington, D.C.; Newark Museum, Newark, New Jersey; New School of Social Research, New York; New York Public Library, New York; Pennsylvania Academy of the Fine Arts, Philadelphia, Pennsylvania; Print Club of Philadelphia, Philadelphia, Pennsylvania; Princeton University, Princeton, New Jersey; Seattle Art Museum, Seattle, Washington; Smith College, Northampton, Massachusetts; University of Delaware, Wilmington, Delaware; University of Nebraska, Lincoln, Nebraska; Whitney Museum of American Art, New York; Worcester Art Museum, Worcester, Massachusetts

Leonard Baskin is represented by the Grace Borgenicht Gallery, New York; the Boris Mirski Gallery, Boston; and the H. Shickman Gallery, New York, for prints

Selected Bibliography

Periodicals
American Artist, 24:6, Oct 1960, "Cover: Football"
———, 30:40, Sept 1966, "Fine Art for an Institutional Series: Container Corporation of America"
Appel, Alfred. "A Note on Baskin." *Sequoia*, Stanford University, Winter 1965
Art Digest, 28:18, June 1954, "Exhibition of Drawings and Woodcuts at Grace Borgenicht Gallery"
———, 28:9, April 15, 1964, "Exhibition of Drawings at Boris Mirski Gallery, Boston"
Art in America, 44, No. 1:48–49, Feb 1956, "New Talent in the USA: with Note by the Artist"
———, 47, No. 4:28–37, Winter 1959, "Artist Printer"
———, 49, No. 4:38, Nov 1961, "Stamps Designed by Fine Artists"
———, 52, No. 6:98, Dec 1964, "Original Christmas Cards"
Art News, 53:74, June 1954, "Exhibition at Borgenicht Gallery"
———, 54:17, Nov 1955, "Shahn/Baskin Collaboration on the Color Wood Engraving: Beatitude"
———, 56:9, March 1957, "Exhibition at Borgenicht Gallery"
———, 57:53, April 1958, "Drawings at Borgenicht"
———, 59:16, May 1960, "Exhibition at Borgenicht Gallery"
———, 60:13, April 1961, "Exhibition at Borgenicht Gallery"
———, 61:46, Summer 1962, "Exhibition at Borgenicht Gallery"
———, 61:12, Feb 1963, "Exhibition at A.A.A. Gallery"
———, 63:14, April 1964, "Exhibition at Borgenicht Gallery"
———, 63:16, Summer 1964, "Exhibition at Borgenicht Gallery"

Achilles Mourning the Death of Patrocles   1967   bronze, 1/5   29 x 32 x 31″

————, 64:17, April 1965, "Exhibition at Borgenicht Gallery"

————, 65:10, March 1966, "Exhibition at Borgenicht Gallery"

————, 66:12, Summer 1967, "Exhibition at Borgenicht Gallery"

Arts, 31:53, March 1957, "Exhibition of Sculpture, Drawings, and Woodcuts at Borgenicht Gallery"

————, 31:8, Sept 1957, "Awarded the O'Hara Museum Prize in the Tokyo Biennial of Prints"

————, 32:64, April 1958, "Drawings at Borgenicht"

————, 34:56, May 1960, "Exhibition at Borgenicht Gallery"

————, 40:53, June 1966, "Exhibition at Borgenicht Gallery"

Ashton, Dore. "Art: Baskin's Foreboding Reflections." *New York Times*, April 2, 1958

————. "A to B: Dore Ashton Answers Leonard Baskin on the Question of Originality in Art." *Studio*, 166:194–97, Nov 1963

————. "Carnival of Materials in Sculpture." St. Louis *Post-Dispatch*, Dec 20, 1964

Ayrton, Michael. "The Sculpture of Leonard Baskin." *Motif*, 10:44, Fall 1962

Baskin, Leonard. "Four Drawings, and an Essay on Kollwitz." *Massachusetts Review*, Oct 1959, pp. 96–104

————. "Necessity for the Image." *Atlantic Monthly*, 207:73–76, April 1961

————. "Of Roots and Veins, A Testimonial." *Atlantic Monthly*, 214:65–68, Sept 1964

————. "On the Nature of Originality." *Show*, August 1963

Burlington Magazine, 100:185, May 1958, "Drawings at the Borgenicht"

Burrows, Carlyle. "New Exhibits: Some Striking Developments in the Graphic Arts." *New York Herald Tribune*, June 6, 1954

————. "Three Kings of Sculpture by Three Modern Artists." *New York Herald Tribune*, March 20, 1960

Canaday, John. "Baskin and the Sooty God." *New York Times*, February 9, 1964

————. "Consider the Common Firefly and the Forest Snail: Book Review." *New York Times*, July 15, 1962

Coates, R. M. "Art Galleries: Exhibition at the Borgenicht." *New Yorker*, 36:116, March 26, 1960

Collings, H. F. "Leonard Baskin, Master of the Woodcut." *Scholastic Arts*, 62:38–39, Nov 1962

Dolbin, B. F. "Kunst: Obdachlose Kunst." *Aufbau*, New York, June 11, 1954

————. "Welt der Kunst." *Aufbau*, New York, May 25, 1962

Domus, 385:11, Dec 1961, "I Premi Alla VI Biennale di San Paolo"

Freundlich, August L. "The Communication of Leonard Baskin." *Motive*, 22:16, Feb 1962

Genauer, Emily. "Familiar and Fresh Baskin." *New York Herald Tribune*, April 2, 1961

————. "A Variety of Printer-Poets." *New York Herald Tribune*, Dec 14, 1963

————. "Young Death to Aged Joy." *New York Herald Tribune*, May 13, 1962

Getlein, Frank. "Gallery of Modern Art Opens Finest Exhibition." *Sunday Star*, Washington, D.C., Sept 22, 1963

Groschwitz, G. Von. "American Prints: A New Phase." *Cincinnati Museum Bulletin*, 7:25, Jan 1962

Gruen, John. "Slaves to Style." *New York Herald Tribune*, Feb 16, 1964

Habitat, 65:34–35, 1961, "VI Bienal de Arte São Paulo: Premios a Artistas Estrangeiros"

Hampshire Gazette, Northampton, Massachusetts, May 7, 1966, "Baskin to Receive Honorary Degree"

Harrison, J. "Exhibition at Borgenicht Gallery." *Arts*, 38:32, April 1964

Heitler, Bruce. "Leonard Baskin: Rebel with a Flare." *Yale Daily News*, New Haven, Connecticut, March 18, 1967

Howard, J. "On Pop Art, Blake and Bohemianism." *Life*, 56:41–42, Jan 24, 1964

Johnson, Una E. "Head of a Poet, 1954." *Brooklyn Museum Bulletin*, 17, No. 2:14, 1956

Kaufman, B. "New Kind of Humanism." *Commonweal*, 72:310–11, June 16, 1961

Kay, Jane. "Baskin's Bird, A Hawkish Dove." *Daily News*, Springfield, Massachusetts, May 18, 1967

Lidman, David. "Thoreau Design by Leonard Baskin." *New York Times*, April 9, 1967

Life, 42:83–84, 87, March 25, 1957, "Images of Mortality"

————, 56:37, Jan 24, 1964, "Pleasant Pariah"

Mitchell, Margaretta. "Leonard Baskin: Animate with Hope." *Ramparts*, 6:46–49, March 1968

Motif, 10:53–60, Winter 1962–1963, "Leonard Baskin"

Newsweek, 60:66, Oct 22, 1962, "They Frighten People: Exhibition at Bowdoin College Museum of Art"

Nielsen, Jeanie. "Baskin Describes Variety of Work." *The Sophian*, Smith College, March 19, 1957

O'Doherty, Brian. "Art: Human Landscape." *New York Times*, April 3, 1961

————. "Leonard Baskin." *Art in America*, 50, No. 2:66–72, Summer 1962

————. "Leonard Baskin." *Art in America*, 51, No. 4:118–23, August 1963

Portland Museum Bulletin, 17:2, January 1956, "Baskin Prints and Drawings: Forthcoming Exhibition"

Preston, S. "On the Other Hand at the Borgenicht Gallery." *Burlington Magazine*, 102 :229, May 1960

Raynor, V. "Exhibition at Borgenicht Gallery." *Arts*, 35 :87, Sept 1962

Rodman, S. "Writer as Collector." *Art in America*, 46, No. 4 :29–31, Summer 1958

Roylance, D. R. "Leonard Baskin's Gehenna Press." *Art in America*, 54, No. 6 :56–59, Nov 1966

Rykwert, A. "A Londra." *Domus*, 392 :53, July 1962

Schiff, Bennett. "In the Art Galleries." *New York Post*, August 18, 1957

Setz, Peter. "Nouvelles Images de l'Homme." *L'Oeil*, No. 62 :50, Feb 1960

Society Hill Newsletter, Philadelphia, March 1966, "Baskin Visits Philadelphia for Sculpture Dedication, Art Exhibition"

Spence, Robert. "Leonard Baskin." *Art Journal*, 22 No. 2 :88–91, Winter 1962–1963

Telegram, Worcester, Massachusetts, May 8, 1960, "Six to Receive Honors at Clark June 5"

Time, 75 :66–67, Jan 18, 1960, "Monumentalist"

Turner, E. H. "Books : the Illustrated Book. Work of Baskin and Town." *Canadian Art*, 20 :136–37, March 1963

Werner, Alfred. "Leonard Baskin : Art for Life's Sake." *American Artist*, 28 :40–45, Nov 1964

———. "Views and Visions." *The Jewish News*, New York, May 5, 1961

Willard, C. "Drawing Today." *Art in America*, 52, No. 5 :49–67, Oct 1964

Exhibition Catalogs (arranged chronologically)

Worcester Art Museum, Worcester, Massachusetts, "Leonard Baskin : Sculpture, Drawings, Woodcuts," November 30, 1956 through January 1, 1957

Museu de Arte Moderna, São Paulo, Brazil VI Bienal, 1961. United States. Text by William S. Lieberman

Museum Boymans-van Beuningen, Rotterdam, Netherlands, "Leonard Baskin : Sculptuur, Tekeningen, Grafiek," May 5 through July 2, 1961. Text by Peter and Thàlia Selz

Royal Watercolor Society Galleries, London, England, "Leonard Baskin /Woodcuts and Wood-Engravings," May 1 to May 26, 1962. Text by Ted Hughes

Bowdoin College Museum of Art, Brunswick, Maine, "Leonard Baskin," 1962. Text by Winslow Ames, Julius S. Held, Harold Joachim, Rico Lebrun, Ray Nash

Film

Forma, Warren. "Images of Leonard Baskin." (1965) 16 mm ; color ; running time 28 minutes. Directed by Warren Forma. Original music by Ernest Pintoff

Small Birdman   1963   bronze   25½ x 11½ x 14¼″

Great Wood Dead Man 1968 wood 31 x 28½ x 16″

Great Man 1964 ink 87 x 42″

Nightmare 1964 ink 77 x 42"

Among the American artists included in the present Biennale, Byron Burford may be the least known in terms of national reputation. Hopefully, the occasion will redress this fact in favor of one of the most considerable accomplishments among our contemporary painters. Burford's lack of fame is, in a large sense, a matter of inclination if not of choice. His first one-man show in New York took place in 1966 only after years of waiting for what appeared to be the right moment for such a step. There is no question of his pre-eminence among the painters active in the American Middle West, and his record as a teacher and an exhibitor is such that he can be identified as an artistic presence of real importance.

His is a personal world, an artist's world, filled with the resonance of actual experience. He moves among his chosen subjects with the ease of a man who has found his truest affinities with the worlds of jazz musicians, migratory workers and, more recently, circus people, explorers, and participants of World War I. These are not in any way unusual subjects; only in the explorers can there be said to be a theme that has been rarely exploited. In all of them one finds a common element—that of a special group of individuals separated from society by dedication to an abstraction, that of the artist to a performance, that of the explorer to the unknown parts of the earth, that of the soldier caught up in a cause. In all these areas of experience, an outwardly dramatic activity contains a strictly disciplined emotion.

For instance, the *Explorers' Dinner* is superbly evocative of the communal experience of dining, a commonplace yet symbolic ritual in the atmosphere of candles and a flag. In *Homage to Clyde*, Burford has seized upon the climactic emotion of the animal act in a tableau of extreme tension, expressed not only in the mutual defiance of trainer and beasts, but also in the excited tonality of the color.

The great looming image of *Mrs. Corsey with Butterflies* is a veritable icon of belief in the ritual and the magic which is contained in the performance of the carnival. This image, like many others in Burford's work, suggests the painted canvas banners which line the carnival midway. This is based on the painter's direct experience in years of summertime employment with the traveling shows of the American Middle West.

Recent criticism has classified Burford as a Pop artist, or at least as an example of the influence of Pop. Although some of his recent pictures may have suggested this in the use of trademarks, lettering, and the like, it is necessary to recognize that he has indulged his liking for such commonplace subject matter for a much longer period than is contained in the entire, brief history of Pop Art, and in his use of such materials he has rarely departed from his instinctive feeling for color as a primary organizing element and for the refinement of the picture surface both tonal and tactile. He is a craftsman in a thoroughly traditional sense. It is accurate, perhaps, to say that he has not remained untouched by the innovations of recent years, but he has used them in his own way, and well within a sensibility that is vastly different.

Biographical Note

Born, Jackson, Mississippi, 1920

Education
1938–1942, State University of Iowa; 1946, Graduate Fellowship, State University of Iowa

Teaching Positions
1947 to present, State University of Iowa; 1959, Visiting Professor, University of Minnesota, Duluth, Minnesota; 1962, Visiting Professor, California College of Arts and Crafts, Oakland, California

One-man Exhibitions
1941, State College of Iowa, Cedar Falls, Iowa; 1951, 1963, State University of Iowa, Iowa City, Iowa; 1958, 1967, Walker Art Center, Minneapolis, Minnesota; 1961, 1967, Des Moines Art Center, Des Moines, Iowa; 1962, Richmond Art Center, Richmond, California; 1962, California College of Arts and Crafts, Oakland, California; 1962, 1963, 1965, Hansen Galleries, San Francisco, California; 1963, Joslyn Art Museum, Omaha, Nebraska; 1964, Distelheim Gallery, Chicago, Illinois; 1964, Cowles Museum, Spokane, Washington; 1964, University of Nebraska, Lincoln, Nebraska; 1964, University of Wisconsin, Madison, Wisconsin; 1964, Sioux City Art Center, Sioux City, Iowa; 1964, Illinois State University, Normal, Illinois; 1965, Ball State University, Muncie, Indiana; 1966, Babcock Galleries, New York; 1966, University of Missouri, Columbia, Missouri; 1967, Northwest Missouri State College, Maryville, Missouri; 1967, Portland State College, Portland, Oregon; 1967, Illinois Wesleyan University, Bloomington, Illinois; 1967, Cherokee Art Center, Cherokee, Iowa; 1968, Creighton University, Omaha, Nebraska; 1968, Waterloo Art Association, Waterloo, Iowa; 1968, Morehead State College, Morehead, Minnesota; 1968, Western Illinois University, Macon, Illinois

Honors and Awards
1946, 1948, 1950, First Prize, Mississippi Art Association, Jackson, Mississippi; 1947, 1948, Julius P. Rosenwald Fellowship; 1960, 1961, John Simon Guggenheim Fellowship; 1961, Ford Foundation

Homage to Clyde   1966   oil on canvas   60 x 60"

Purchase Award, Des Moines Art Center, Biennial Exhibition; 1963, Iowa University Research Fellowship; 1964, Ford Foundation Purchase Award, William Rockhill Nelson Gallery of Art, Kansas City, Missouri

Public Collections

American Republic Insurance Company, Des Moines, Iowa; Atlanta Art Association, Atlanta, Georgia; Ball State University, Muncie, Indiana; Brooks Memorial Art Gallery, Memphis, Tennessee; Colorado Springs Fine Art Center, Colorado Springs, Colorado; Cowles Museum, Spokane, Washington; Davenport Municipal Art Gallery, Davenport, Iowa; Des Moines Art Center, Des Moines, Iowa; First National Bank Collection, Minneapolis, Minnesota; Illinois Wesleyan University, Bloomington, Illinois; Joslyn Art Museum, Omaha, Nebraska; J. S. Guggenheim Foundation, New York; Kansas State University, Manhattan, Kansas; MacNider Museum, Mason City, Iowa; Queens University, Kingston, Ontario, Canada; Rockford Art Association, Rockford, Illinois; St. Paul Art Center, St. Paul, Minnesota; Sioux City Art Center, Sioux City, Iowa; Springfield Art Museum, Springfield, Missouri; State College of Iowa, Cedar Falls, Iowa; State University of Iowa, Iowa City, Iowa; University of Hartford, Hartford, Connecticut; University of Minnesota, Duluth, Minnesota; University of Nebraska, Lincoln, Nebraska; Walker Art Center, Minneapolis, Minnesota; Washburn University, Topeka, Kansas; William Rockhill Nelson Gallery of Art, Kansas City, Missouri

Byron Burford is represented by the Babcock Galleries, New York

Selected Bibliography

Periodicals

Arnason, H. H. "Recent Art of the Upper Midwest; Universities as Centers of Art." *Art in America*, 42, No. 1:44–45, 1954

Art News, 65:15, May 1966, "Exhibition at Babcock Gallery"

Bredt, Theodore. "War and Byron Burford." *San Francisco Chronicle*, Sept 8, 1963

Brown, Richard L. "Compassion and Skill Form His Art." *Kansas City Star*, Sept 26, 1965

Fagan, Beth. "Artist Voices Concern." *Sunday Oregonian*, Portland, Oregon, April 13, 1964

Getlein, Frank. "Art: Pop Turned into Serious Uses in Burford's Work." *Washington Star*, Washington, D.C., Nov 5, 1967

———. "Where Do We Go From Here?" *New Republic*, pp. 34–35, Nov 2, 1963

Haggie, Helen. "Gallery Acquires Four Pieces." *Lincoln Evening Journal*, Lincoln, Nebraska, Aug 2, 1963

Iowa City Press-Citizen, Iowa City, Iowa, April 2, 1966, "U.I. Artist Byron Burford Has Exhibition in New York"

Kind, Joshua. "Girlie Art Turned into a Highly Formal Image." *Chicago Daily News*, June 18, 1966

Milwaukee Journal, Jan 25, 1959, "Fine Art Shows Stretch the Walls at Beloit"

Moen, Gwen. "Nash, Burford Exhibitions at Tweed Gallery Reviewed." *Umd Statesman*, Duluth, Minnesota, Jan 17, 1964

Moul, Francis. "Painter Burford Dissects Course of Art Since 1900's." *Sioux City Journal*, March 16, 1964

New York Herald Tribune, April 9, 1966, "Byron Burford, Prominent Midwestern American Artist, Opens in New York Debut Exhibition at Babcock Galleries"

Waterloo Sunday Courier, Waterloo, Iowa, April 8, 1962, "Burford Show at Center"

Exhibition Catalogs (arranged chronologically)

Tweed Gallery, University of Minnesota. "Byron Burford." January 1964. Text by Orazio Fumagalli

Sioux City Art Center Association. "Byron Burford Exhibition." March 5 through March 29, 1964

Babcock Galleries, New York. "New York Debut Exhibition, Byron Burford." April 4 through April 23, 1966

Fine Arts Center, University of Missouri. "Byron Burford, Exhibition of Paintings and Drawings." September 12 through October 7, 1966

George Washington University Art Gallery, Washington, D.C. "Byron Burford Exhibition." October 4 through November 6, 1967. Text by D. H. Teller

Explorers' Dinner, No. 2 1966 oil on canvas 57¾ x 56¾"

Mrs. Corsey with Butterflies   1967   oil and plastic on canvas   100 x 81″

Jack Earl and Friends   1967   oil and serigraph on canvas   80″ diameter

Robert Cremean's sculpture is supremely personal. It is undeniably Cubist in form, Expressionist in feeling, and is related to these sources in a way which, though indirect, is completely assimilated without self-consciousness. More particularly, there are also echoes of a thoroughly baroque involvement with form in its envelope of light and space. The informing spirit of his work is a mood of disenchantment intrinsically characteristic of the present, a convoluted, mysterious, and evocative concern with self-understanding.

In many of his works there is an exploration of the basic relationships of one figure to another which, at first glance, appear to carry no more meaning than is implied in the purely formal aspects of the problem. However, there is again an undertone of seriousness, of psychological complication which at times has the stately nuance of dance or participation in a ritual, and at other times shifts toward a dramatic situation of perceptible intensity. This containment of feeling is even stronger in the many compositions which involve the single figure and an additional element of setting, consisting of a chair, or bed, or platform which is, variously, the couch of an odalisque, the table of a dissection, or the bath of Marat. There are also a number of seated figures enthroned on chairs of processional richness and complexity. The observer approaches these works with a sense of entrance into a situation, of involvement, participation, or witness. This quality is particularly and powerfully noticeable in the Marat series, and again in the series of anatomy lessons, where the impact pushes one's response well past instinctive revulsion into a heightened awareness which fuses both seeing and understanding.

Another notable quality in the work of Robert Cremean is his linearism. His uncanny spatial sense grasps the massed structure of the human body, but rarely suggests anatomy as such. Purists in such matters can be extremely unhappy with Cremean's inventions. Still they work, and are marvelously suggestive of bone, tissue, and muscle without a single merely descriptive touch. Gesture, inclination, attitude are seized with an accuracy that imbues the whole work with a telling actuality. In *Anatomy Lesson No. 4*, for instance, the trunk rests on its side in a half turn that reveals the back of the figure, tautly responsive to the experience of dissection. This understanding of the movement of bodies is most notably revealed through his sense of drawing, which is frequently implied, often demonstrated. From his earliest work Cremean has used the device of drawing on the sculptured form but it has increased in its frequency and emphasis in recent years. In his *Fragment For a Disputed Curia* of 1962 and the large drawing on wood simply titled *Curia* of 1963, the relationship of drawing and carving reached a verge of crisis where the two works were, in a way, mirrors of each other. In the more recent hinged panels of 1966, one of which, the *Studies for a Self-Portrait and a Self-Portrait*, is included in the exhibition. Cremean has accomplished a *tour de force*. Large-scale figures, some in pure line, some totally drawn, occupy the surface in an astonishing play of dimensional effects. The actual carving is minimal, and its effect is that of a highlight, throwing the whole into a special frame of reference in a sort of optical play, far removed from the assault and battery kind of experience which has become the commonplace of recent optical art. Lastly, in this matter of drawing, there is Cremean's command of contour, which has a flow and a volumetric fullness of truly sculptural quality. Sometimes seen in silhouette, sometimes in shadow, sometimes in the void of negative space, the outline becomes a kind of drawing in space.

Cremean is a virtuoso technician, but his command of means is always subordinated to meaning. There are few American sculptors with so pronounced a gift for color and texture. The massive laminations rich in inlays and stripings and the yielding or resisting textures of the various woods with which the artist begins are in themselves the most astounding forecasts of the completed work. His surfaces are detailed with chisel work of the utmost finesse, suggesting flesh and bone, yet they are always superbly natural and of the material. He has worked with the conventional repertory of media including terra cotta and bronze, but he has concentrated most particularly within a range of individual woodworking techniques. These are variously described as wood mortise, wood maché, or lamination combined with metal, cloth, and plaster. Within the past several years he has added to the natural color effects of the materials by painting or toning surfaces or areas with flat, unambiguous colors, black, white, and a vulgar pink, as in the short series of *Whores* done in 1966.

Most recently in the masterly lithography of *The Fourteen Stations of the Cross*, Cremean has extended his abilities in a major way, achieving not only an outstanding use of the medium and a genuinely original use of color, but a deeply moving embodiment of a traditional theme as well.

Biographical Note

Born, Toledo, Ohio, September 28, 1932

Education
1950–1952, Alfred University; 1954, Cranbrook Academy of Arts; 1954, Italy; 1956, Cranbrook Academy of Arts, M.F.A.

Teaching Positions
1956, Detroit Institute of Art, Detroit, Michigan; 1956, University of California at Los Angeles, California; 1957, La Jolla Museum of Art, La Jolla, California

One-man Exhibitions
1955, Schneider Gallery, Rome, Italy; 1955, Cranbrook Museum, Bloomfield Hills, Michigan; 1958, 1959, Paul Kantor Gallery, Los Angeles, California; 1960 through 1967, Esther Robles Gallery, Los Angeles, California; 1962, Santa Barbara Museum, Santa Barbara, California; 1962, California Palace of the Legion of Honor, San Francisco, California; 1964, University of Nebraska, Lincoln, Nebraska; 1964, University of Texas, Austin, Texas; 1965, University of Colorado, Boulder, Colorado; 1965, Fort Worth Art Center, Fort Worth, Texas; 1965, State University of Iowa, Iowa City, Iowa; 1966, University of Illinois, Champaign-Urbana, Illinois; 1966, The Municipal Art Department, Barnsdall Galleries, Los Angeles, California; 1966, Marin County Museum, San Rafael, California; 1966, The Visalia College of the Sequoia, Sequoia, California; 1966, Fullerton Junior College, Fullerton, California; 1966, Southwest College, Chula Vista, California; 1967, University of California at Santa Barbara, California; 1967, California State College, Domengus Hills, California; 1967, San Bernardino Visual Arts Center, San Bernardino, California; 1967, San Luis Obispo Civic Arts Association, San Luis Obispo, California; 1967, Sacramento California State Fair, Sacramento, California; 1967, California Art Commission, Sacramento, California; 1967, Alan Hancock College, Santa Maria, California; 1967, Redlands University, Redlands, California; 1967, Chabot College, Hayward, California; 1967, Downey Museum, Downey, California; 1967, Ceritos College, Norwalk, California; 1967, Valley Shore College, Burbank, California; 1967, San Fernando Valley State College, Northridge, California; 1968, Landau-Alan Gallery, New York

Honors and Awards
1954, Fulbright Scholarship; 1966–1967, Tamarind Workshop Fellowship

Public Collections
City Art Museum, St. Louis, Missouri; Detroit Institute of Arts, Detroit, Michigan; Los Angeles County Museum of Art, Los Angeles, California; Santa Barbara Museum of Art, Santa Barbara, California; Toledo Museum of Art, Toledo, Ohio; University of California at Los Angeles, Los Angeles, California; University of Miami, Miami, Florida; University of Nebraska, Lincoln, Nebraska

Robert Cremean is represented by the Felix Landau Gallery, Los Angeles, California and the Landau-Alan Gallery, New York

Selected Bibliography

Periodicals
Art in America, 49, No. 1:40–41, 1961, "New Talent USA: Sculpture"
Art News, 56:66, Jan 1957, "Exhibition of Sculpture, Plaques and Wash Drawings at the Paul Kantor Gallery, Los Angeles"
———, 57:53, March 1958, "Los Angeles: New Work at the Paul Kantor Gallery"
Arts, 32:20, Feb 1958, "Los Angeles, Exhibition at Paul Kantor's"
Grafton, Samuel. "Tamarind, Where Artist and Craftsman Meet." *Lithopinion 5*, II No. 1, 1967
Langsner, J. "Exhibition in Los Angeles." *Art News*, 58:60, June 1959
———. "Exhibition at Esther Robles Gallery, Los Angeles." *Art News*, 61:52, Oct 1962
———. "Los Angeles." *Art News*, 65:57, Feb 1967
Millier, Arthur. "Cremean Sculpture Stirs Extraordinary Excitement." *Los Angeles Times*, Feb 23, 1958
Perkins, C. M. "Los Angeles: The Way You Look at It." *Art in America*, 54, No. 2:117, March 1966

Secunda, A. "Artist as Craftsman—Craftsman as Artist, Fine Arts Pavilion Newport Harbor, California." *Craft Horizons*, 24:43, Jan 1964

Seldis, Henry J. "Cremean Sculpture Impresses." *Los Angeles Times*, Dec 13, 1965

———. "Southern California." *Art in America*, 48, No. 4:57, Winter 1960

Wholden, R. G. "Exhibition at Esther Robles Gallery." *Arts*, 38:42, Nov 1963

Exhibition Catalogs (arranged chronologically)

Paul Kantor Gallery, Beverly Hills, California, "Robert Cremean," February 17 through March 14, 1958

Paul Kantor Gallery, Beverly Hills, California, "Robert Cremean," March 23 through April 17, 1959

Esther Robles Gallery, Los Angeles, California, "Recent Sculpture of Robert Cremean," April 11 through April 30, 1960

Esther Robles Gallery, Los Angeles, California, "Robert Cremean, Sculpture Exhibition" (traveling exhibition), April 1 through July 1, 1961

Los Angeles Municipal Art Department, "The Image Retained" (traveling exhibition), May 30 through September 4, 1961. Organized by Henry J. Seldis

Esther Robles Gallery, Los Angeles, California, "Robert Cremean, Recent Sculpture," July 2 through July 28, 1962

Esther Robles Gallery, Los Angeles, California, "Robert Cremean, Recent Sculpture," September 9 through October 12, 1963

Esther Robles Gallery, Los Angeles, California, "Robert Cremean Sculpture Exhibition" (traveling exhibition), September 1964 through March 1966

Esther Robles Gallery, Los Angeles, California, "Robert Cremean, Recent Sculpture," December 6 through December 31, 1965

California Arts Commission, "The Sculpture of Robert Cremean" (traveling exhibition), December 6 through September 4, 1966–1967

Landau-Alan Gallery, New York, "Robert Cremean," May 7 through May 29, 1968

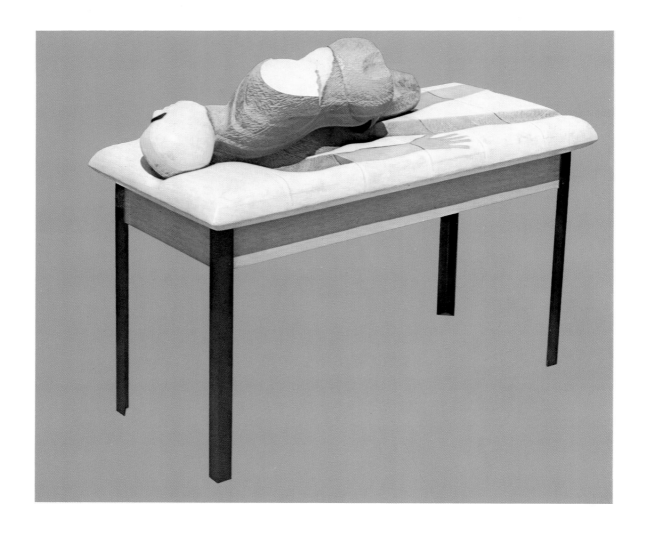

The Anatomy Lesson No. 4   1965   laminated wood, metal   53 x 66 x 30″

Studies for a Self-Portrait and a Self-Portrait   1966   wood, oil, graphite   80 x 60″ closed ; 80 x 120″ open

Sibyl 1967 laminated wood 44¼ x 36 x 24″

Edwin Dickinson is an artist apart. He is at once traditional and experimental, conservative and radical, committed and nonaligned. He is unique in one respect if in no other, for he is widely admired among his artistic colleagues of both the academy, where he belongs by right of election, and the avant-garde, where he belongs by mutual affinity. Like others of his generation, Marin, Davis, and Hopper, he has always been his own man, perhaps even more wholly so than any of them; like American artists before him, Homer, Ryder, or Eakins, there is in him a deep vein of old-fashioned Yankee independence, an impressive capacity for finding out for himself what it is that he wants to do. More particularly, he might well be placed in that special company of American visionaries, Ryder, Blakelock, C. S. Price, whose independence was well founded on open, varied, and commonplace experiences, but whose preference was to remain within a strictly personal view of those experiences, which, on the whole, coincided little or not at all with the conventional view. Dickinson, like these other painters, knows of the rightness and the wrongness of things as defined by society but chooses instead, with stubborn conviction, the rightness and wrongness of things as he sees them, which means as revealed to him by intuition, memory, dream, and the abstract methods of science and music. There has been no artistic imagination so complete, so visual, so instinctive since Ryder's, which was fed by a love of Wagner and Shakespeare. In Dickinson there is an equal reservoir of feeling fed by Proust and Joyce.

That part of Dickinson which is explained in terms of education and travel is not particularly unusual ; the instruction to which he exposed himself was of the conventional kind, including work with William Merritt Chase in New York, Charles W. Hawthorne on Cape Cod, and Frank Vincent DuMond at the Art Students League. This was climaxed by a year of instruction at the Académie de la Grande Chaumière in Paris, and travel in Spain, where he discovered El Greco, Zurbarán, and Velasquez. He acknowledges that Hawthorne, a teacher of more than ordinary skill, was of most importance to him during these educative experiences.

Beyond this point, the development of Dickinson's art has been astoundingly free of any relationship to the so-called mainstream. Through the decades of The Eight, early abstraction, Regionalism and Social Consciousness, Expressionism and Surrealism, and lastly the dramatic ten or fifteen years of Abstract Expressionism, Dickinson has been producing a body of work which relates to all these events only in the most general way. Nevertheless, in this half century of self-centered activity he has encompassed much of what other American artists were seeking to achieve in a much more public way and in many instances with much less complete success. With the exception, admittedly a large one, of pure abstraction, which was the most important achievement of the forties and fifties, Dickinson has touched upon almost every other problem of consequence, but in his own time and in his own way.

The series of major pictures, beginning with the *Rival Beauties* of 1915 and including *Interior* (1916), *An Anniversary* (1921), *The Cello Player* (1924–26), *The Fossil Hunters* (1926–28), *Woodland Scene* (1929–35), *Composition with Still Life* (1933–37), and *Ruin at Daphne* (1943–53), constitutes one of the most impressive explorations of twentieth-century pictorial form by any American painter. It is sufficient to say that there have been no other pictures like them in American art.

It was not possible to bring two of the finest pictures in the series to Venice,* but in those which are here one can see the full scope of this extraordinary imagination at work. *An Anniversary* consists of a great dense pyramid of forms, an old man, a girl, a musician, set in a space filled with other figures, male and female. At the base of the picture is an array of still-life detail : decorated dishes, a tureen, a pitcher, a vase, a Mozart score. Dickinson has stated that the picture is not a depiction of an event. Its title was applied afterward and refers to nothing whatever. This is typical. There is no narrative intention, no literary explanation, only forms and objects, selected and arranged for a purely visual delectation, the quality of this pleasure being determined by the glossy richness of the color, deeply shadowed through a range of blues, greens, and browns, and the mysterious visual placement of the forms in the space. They pile up and seem to float in a kind of liquid suspension. This is a discerning use of the idea of cubism, if we assume that Dickinson was in any way aware of it, and it shows far more understanding of the idea than is the case in the work of any number of other Americans who were grappling with it at the same time.

The Cello Player is even more assured in its daring. Here the picture space is like a deep bowl, with the single figure poised near the forward edge. The usual array of enamelled pots, books, shells, musical instruments, and that signature motif, a full-blown

---

*The Fossil Hunters, Whitney Museum of American Art, and *Composition with Still Life*, Museum of Modern Art, New York.

rose placed in a sequence of the subtlest relationship, surround the cellist in a circling arrangement of shapes and forms, which if perceived purely as such, constitute a kind of visual accompaniment to the solemn simplicity of the cellist and his instrument.

The *Woodland Scene* marks the opening up of the series to combine the mysterious figure with the mysterious landscape. Here the relationship takes on the quality of phantasm. There are juxtaposed figures of two women, one of them old, dressed in a voluminous coat and surrounded with luxurious drapery, the other floating head downward, with head, shoulders, and breast bared to the dazzling light which emanates from a pillar of fire that dominates the right side of the picture and seems to contain a third figure, a female nude. The environment is that of a forest: in the foreground a broken masonry wall, on one side a ploughshare, on the other part of a cartwheel, propped up against a clump of trees. It is impossible to interpret the picture in any conventional way. This is an internal imagery, whether of dream or hallucination. It is pure romantic imagination, the free invention of psychology and emotion. One is reminded of such artists as Fuseli or, in our own tradition, of William Rimmer.

Dickinson's *Stranded Brig* of 1934 is a part of this group of pictures, although both the subject and the composition are of a different kind than any of those just discussed. This picture was painted under the Federal Arts Project of the nineteen-thirties. Out of the many thousands of canvases executed, this must be one of the comparatively few of high quality. Dickinson has always had a deep interest in the sea, in the professions of the fisherman and the sailor, and in the heroic history of arctic exploration. He has painted a number of pictures having to do with this subject. *Stranded Brig* is a sea picture that is very far removed from the specific tradition of such images, yet it has in it all the wildness and terror of marine disaster.

As a climax to these pictures, painted over a period of fifteen or twenty years, there is *Ruin at Daphne*, which in itself required nine years to complete. This is the artist's best known work and not without reason. As the early fantasias, and even the more recent landscapes, are not quite like anything else in twentieth-century American painting, so the *Ruin at Daphne* stands out, by itself, within the body of the artist's work. Besides the sea, another of Dickinson's enthusiasms is the architecture of the classical past, which he has explored repeatedly during his travels abroad. From his travels he has chosen to invent his own historical graph in a complex of buildings which are purely imaginary, but based primarily on Roman buildings of the 1st, 2nd, and 3rd centuries A.D. In the upper left section of the picture there is a distinct echo of the temple of Venus at Baalbek. The history of the picture's execution is in a striking way an imaginative capsule of historical process, of planning, construction, reconstruction, and destruction. Figures and a self-portrait came and went, and the whole repertory of the artist's favorite motifs was tried and discarded. Even his love of the ancient fabric was not so strong that he could resist the inspiration of a purely Dickinsonian pillar supporting a cantilevered stairway that rises out of the depths of the picture, like an invention by Piranesi. The whole echoing precinct is inhabited only by a few fluttering birds on the edge of a fountain. Perhaps the taste for ruins seems *retardataire*, but it is undeniably of interest when a creative contemporary can look at such sites as Baalbek or Leptis Magna and see them not in any antiquarian sense at all, but in the abstract sense that is peculiarly ours. A comparison with another famous American picture, Peter Blume's *Eternal City* of 1934–37, will underline the strictly visual quality of Dickinson's picture.

After *Ruin at Daphne*, no subsequent work has developed on a comparable scale of complexity. Indeed, a whole sequence of pictures of quite a different character, which had actually been begun some ten years before, presents a second Edwin Dickinson.

This sequence is made up of small canvases, executed *au premier coup*, as Dickinson himself refers to it. This method avoids the laborious building of the picture over a period of years and concentrates instead on a spontaneous seizure of the chosen subject in the briefest time and with the most direct technique. Some of these paintings are baffling on first contact, for the seeming imprecision is the result of a delicately registered effect, a kind of summing up in terms that come miraculously close to total abstraction. The many small pictures done on Cape Cod, in Brittany and Southern France, are all of this kind. They have a quality of light and texture which, in the Cape Cod pictures, is bleached with fog and blank stretches of sand and sky, and in the French pictures suggests rather the dense, ripe heat of late summer. In these works, too, we find him choosing the simplest motif, a rock on the beach, a flapping flag on a neighbor's house, the view from a porch or window, not infrequently with a straight vertical division of the canvas near the center. These are pictures of light, or of sky, or, taken together, of space.

To be sure, there are variants, such as the frequent self-portraits, or portraits of family and friends, nudes, Parisian scenes, and still lifes. Dickinson's ability as a portrait painter is considerable, but the problems appear to challenge him most in the self-portraits and the likenesses of his family. The self-portraits are of special interest. The finest of them belongs to the National Academy of Design, but there is also the remarkable *Self-Portrait in Uniform* (1942) and another (1947), part of the Halperin Collection, in which the face is shadowed by a large leaf.

The recognition given Edwin Dickinson has been slow and late. He has enjoyed that dubious distinction of being a painter's painter for most of his career. The reasons are not all that difficult to determine. The man's independence, which is his most powerful resource, has worked against his fame. He has never participated in any conspicuous way in events, movements, or organizations. In a secondary, but not unimportant sense, his career developed at a moment in our art history when the chief artistic concerns of the day were directed toward objectives of a more critical, perhaps a more revolutionary, nature. The peculiar character of Dickinson's art has little in common with the communal fever of abstract expressionism. It is not without significance that Dickinson's first real break-through took place with the large retrospective exhibition organized by the Graham Gallery in New York in 1961. It came at precisely the moment when an interest in figuration on the part of both artist and public appeared to be a respectable possibility once again. By the time of the Whitney Museum's exhibition in 1965, this interest was a confirmed fact, and Dickinson became a really important figure for the first time.

It is surely time to recognize that his is a visual sensibility of extraordinary scope. It is reactive to experience in objective ways that are as close as anything we have in our art to a purely formal achievement; at the same time his subjectivity is such that he is one of the few Americans to have realized in his work the innocence, the surreality, the exaltation of children, madmen, and poets.*

---

*The "children, madmen, and poets" above is a formulation by Roland F. Pease, which appeared in *Art, U.S.A., Now* (New York, 1963) volume I, pp. 54–57. I trust I have not misunderstood it, for it seemed to me one of the few statements about Dickinson which provide the proper clue to understanding. N.A.G.

Biographical Note

Born, Seneca Falls, New York, 1891

Education
1910–1911, Pratt Institute, New York; 1911–1913, Art Students League, New York, studies with William Merritt Chase and Frank V. DuMond; 1912–1914, studies with Charles W. Hawthorne, Provincetown, Massachusetts

Teaching Positions
1916, Buffalo Academy of Fine Arts, Buffalo, New York; 1922–1923, Art Students League, New York; 1929–1930, Provincetown Art Association, Provincetown, Massachusetts; 1939, Art Institute of Buffalo, Buffalo, New York; 1940, Association for Music and Art, Centerville, Massachusetts; 1940, Wellesley College, Wellesley, Massachusetts; 1940–1941, Stuart School, Boston, Massachusetts; 1941, Association of Music and Art, Cape Cod, Massachusetts; 1942, Wellesley College, Wellesley, Massachusetts; 1945–1949, The Cooper Union for the Advancement of Science and Art, New York; 1945–1961, Art Students League, New York; 1946–1947, Midtown School, New York; 1950, Pratt Institute, New York; 1950–1958, Art School of Brooklyn Museum, Brooklyn, New York; 1951, Dennis Foundation, Dennis, Massachusetts; 1957, visiting instructor, Cornell University, Ithaca, New York; 1957, visiting instructor, Columbia University, New York; 1961, visiting instructor, Boston University, Boston, Massachusetts; 1963–1965, Art Students League, New York

Exhibitions
1919, Exhibition of American painters at the Luxembourg Palace, Paris; 1927, One-man exhibition, Albright Art Gallery, Buffalo, New York; 1928, Carnegie International, Pittsburgh; 1936–1943, Passedoit Gallery, New York; 1939, One-man exhibition, Wood Memorial Gallery, Provincetown, Massachusetts; 1941, One-man exhibition, Stuart School, Boston, Massachusetts; 1942, One-man exhibition, Farnsworth Museum, Wellesley College, Wellesley, Massachusetts; 1943, One-man exhibition, Nantucket Museum, Nantucket, Massachusetts; 1952, "Fifteen Americans," Museum of Modern Art, New York; 1958, Retrospective exhibition, Cushman Gallery, Houston, Texas; 1961, Retrospective exhibition, Graham Gallery, New York; 1961, One-man exhibition, Philadelphia Art Alliance, Philadelphia; 1961, One-man circulating exhibition, Museum of Modern Art, New York; 1965, One-man exhibition, Graham Gallery, New York; 1965, One-man exhibition, Gilman Gallery, New York; 1965, Retrospective exhibition, Whitney Museum of American Art, New York; 1965, One-man exhibition, Syracuse University, Syracuse, New York; 1965, Two-man exhibition, Kansas City Art Institute, Kansas City, Missouri; 1966, One-man exhibition, Katonah Gallery, Katonah, New York; 1966, Two-man exhibition, Pennsylvania Academy of the Fine Arts, Philadelphia; 1967, One-man exhibition, Hawthorne Memorial Gallery, Provincetown Art Association, Provincetown, Massachusetts

Honors and Awards
1929, Second Altman Prize for Figure for "The Fossil Hunters"; 1948, Elected Associate of National Academy of Design; 1949, First Prize for Portrait for "Self-Portrait," National Academy of Design; 1950, Elected Academician of National Academy of Design; 1954, Grant, National Institute of Arts and Letters; 1956, Elected member of National Institute of Arts and Letters; 1956, Medal for Art, The Century Association; 1958, Second Prize for Landscape for "View from Window," National Academy of Design; 1958–1960, Vice-President, National Institute of Arts and Letters; 1959, Grant, Ford Foundation; 1959, Creative Arts Award Medal, Brandeis University; 1961, Elected member, American Academy of Arts and Letters; 1961, Honorary Doctor of Fine Arts, Pratt Institute; 1965, Brevoort-Eickemeyer Prize, Columbia University, New York

Public Collections
Art Institute of Chicago, Chicago, Illinois; Atlanta University, Atlanta, Georgia; Bowdoin College, Brunswick, Maine; Brooklyn Museum, Brooklyn, New York; Commerce Trust Company, Kansas City, Missouri; Joseph H. Hirshhorn Collection, New York; Kansas City Art Institute and School of Design, Kansas City, Missouri; National Academy of Design, New York; Nebraska Art Association, Lincoln, Nebraska; Metropolitan Museum of Art, New York; Museum of Modern Art, New York; Sara Roby Foundation, New York; Springfield Museum of Fine Arts, Springfield, Massachusetts; University of Nebraska, Lincoln, Nebraska; Cornell University, Ithaca, New York; Whitney Museum of American Art, New York

Edwin Dickinson is represented by the Graham Gallery, New York

Selected Bibliography

Books

Dickinson, Edwin. "Introduction" for *Hawthorne on Painting*, edited by Mrs. Charles W. Hawthorne. New York, Dover Publications, Inc., 1960

Goodrich, Lloyd. *The Drawings of Edwin Dickinson*. New Haven, Connecticut, Yale University Press, 1963

Miller, Dorothy. "Edwin Dickinson," from *New Art in America*. Greenwich, Connecticut, New York Graphic Society, 1957

Periodicals

Art Digest, 4:5–6, Nov 15, 1929, "Academy Hangs Prize Work Sideways, Gets Yards of Publicity"

———, 10:19, Feb 1, 1936, "Drawings by Edwin Dickinson"

———, 12:13, April 15, 1938, "The Visions of Edwin Dickinson, 'Lone Spirit'"

———, 15:19, April 1, 1941, "Nostalgic Mysticism of Edwin Dickinson"

Art News, 48:41, Dec 1949, "Reviews and Previews"

———, 54:47, March 1955, "America, 1953; for the Metropolitan"

———, 57:5+, Jan 1959, "The Year's Best"

———, 58:8, April 1959, "Dickinson Retrospective"

Arts, 40:42, Dec 1965, "Exhibition at Whitney Museum"

———, 40:58, Dec 1965, "Exhibition at Graham Gallery"

Art Students League News, Feb 16, 1950, "Edwin Dickinson"

———, March 1959, "Edwin Dickinson Wins Ford Foundation Grant of $10,000"

———, Jan 1962, "Edwin Dickinson Named to American Academy"

Ashton, Dore. "Review of Retrospective at the Graham Gallery." *Arts and Architecture*, 78:4, April 1961

Bird, Paul. "Dickinson's Vapors." *Art Digest*, 13:19, April 15, 1939

Boswell, Helen. "Poetic Edwin Dickinson." *Art Digest*, 16:23, March 15, 1942

Campbell, Lawrence. "Three Painters of Interior Light." *Art News*, 59:47–49+, Feb 1961

Canaday, John. "One City and One Painter." *New York Times*, Oct 24, 1965

Clark, Eliot. "Edwin Dickinson." *Studio*, 162:138–40+, Oct 1961

Coates, Robert. "Art Galleries: Exhibition at the Graham Gallery." *New Yorker*, 37:113–14, Feb 18, 1961

DeKooning, Elaine. "Dickinson and Kiesler." *Art News*, 51:20–23, April 1952

———. "Edwin Dickinson Paints a Picture." *Art News*, 48:26–28, Sept 1949

Devree, Howard. "Around New York." *Magazine of Art*, 33:300, May 1940

———. "Four Solos." *Magazine of Art*, 31:309, May 1938

———. "Work by Edwin Dickinson." *New York Times*, April 16, 1939

Hamilton, Ann. "Current Drawings by Four Artists." *Art News*, 34:7, Feb 15, 1936

Hatch, Robert. "At the Tip of Cape Cod." *Horizon*, 3:28–29, July 1961

Kent, Norman. "Book Notes: The Drawings of Edwin Dickinson." *American Artist*, 28:12, Oct 1964

Kuh, Katharine. "Art Without Isms." *Saturday Review*, 44:37+, March 4, 1961

Lane, James W. "New Exhibitions of the Week." *Art News*, 36:11, April 30, 1938

———. "New Exhibitions of the Week." *Art News*, 37:14, April 15, 1939

———. "New Exhibitions of the Week." *Art News*, 38:16, Dec 16, 1939

———. "New Exhibitions of the Week." *Art News*, 39:14, April 13, 1940

———. "The Passing Show." *Art News*, 40:33, April 1–14, 1941

———. "The Passing Show." *Art News*, 41:26, March 15–30, 1942

Literary Digest, 103:21, Nov 30, 1929, "What is the Right Side Up of a Picture?"

McBride, Henry. "Integrity in Art." *New York Herald Tribune*, April 5, 1941

New York Herald Tribune, July 17, 1936, "Villa la Mouette"

———, April 21, 1940, "Edwin Dickinson" (exhibition notice)

———, Dec 2, 1961, "Academy of Arts, Letters Names Hocking, Dickinson"

New York Times, Dec 6, 1961, "Philosopher and Painter Honored"

Pease, Roland F. "Dickinson." *Art International*, 3:63, April 1961

Porter, Fairfield. "Exhibition at the Graham Gallery." *Nation*, 192:175, Feb 25, 1961

Rondell, Lester. "Letter to the Editor." *Art News*, 48:6, Nov 1949

Schuyler, James. "U.S. Painters Today: Edwin Dickinson." *Portfolio and Art News Annual*, 88–103, 1960

Smith, Jacob Getlar. "Edwin Dickinson, American Mystic." *American Artist*, 21:54–59+, Jan 1957

Tillim, Sidney. "Month in Review." *Arts*, 35:46–48, March 1961

Time, 77:60, Feb 10, 1961, "Defying Time and Fashion"

South Wellfleet Inn   1950   oil on canvas   33¼ x 43⅝″

Waldman, D. "Dickinson : Reality of Reflection." *Art News*, 64 :28–31, Nov 1965
Watson, Forbes. "The Carnegie International." *Arts*, 14 :258, Nov 1928

Exhibition Catalogs (arranged chronologically)

Buffalo Fine Arts Academy, Albright Art Gallery, Buffalo, New York, "An Exhibition of Paintings by Edwin Dickinson," April 17 through May 15, 1927
Rochester Memorial Art Gallery, Rochester, New York, "Edwin Dickinson Exhibition," April 1939
Museum of Modern Art, New York, "Romantic Painting in America," 1943
Museum of Modern Art, New York, "Fifteen Americans," 1952
Andrew Dickson White Museum of Art, Cornell University, Ithaca, New York, "Edwin Dickinson," 1957
The Cushman Gallery, Houston, Texas, "Edwin Dickinson Retrospective," March 30 through April 25, 1958
Atlanta University Art Gallery, Atlanta, Georgia, "Edwin Dickinson," 1959
Boston University Art Gallery, Boston, Massachusetts, "Edwin Dickinson Retrospective Exhibition," March 7 through April 4, 1959
Rose Art Gallery, Brandeis University, Waltham, Massachusetts, "Art on Campus," 1959
Graham Gallery, New York, "Edwin Dickinson Retrospective," February 1 through March 1, 1961
Whitney Museum of American Art, New York, "Edwin Dickinson," October 20 through November 28, 1965. Text by Lloyd Goodrich
Brooklyn Museum of Art, Brooklyn, New York, "The Herbert A. Goldstone Collection of American Art," 1965
Bowdoin College Museum of Art, Brunswick, Maine, "Collecting Privately," no date

An Anniversary 1921 oil on canvas 72 x 60″

The Cello Player   1924/26   oil on canvas   60 x 48¼"

Girl on Tennis Court   1926   oil on panel   36 x 30″

Woodland Scene   1929/35   oil on canvas   71⅜ x 68½"

Rock of Port Issol, West Side   1938   oil on canvas   23 x 28″

Villa Marie-Jeanne   1938   oil on canvas   23¾ x 28¾″

Slanting Apple Tree   1938   oil on canvas   23 x 28″

Nude Figure Prone on Side　1939　oil on canvas　23½ x 29″

Cottage Porch in Reflection   1940   oil on canvas   15 x 21″

Shiloh 1940 oil on canvas 36 x 32″

Constant 1941 oil on canvas 23⅞ x 29″

Ruin at Daphne 1943/53 oil on canvas 48 x 60¼"

The Flag at Frazier's House   1947   oil on canvas   12 x 10″

Self-Portrait   1949   oil on canvas   23 x 20″

Rock, Cape Poge 1950   oil on canvas   12 x 14½″   (oval)

Carousel Bridge, Paris 1952 oil on board 12 x 14½"

Windows, Paris   1952   oil on canvas   12 x 16″

Window and Oar 1955 oil on board 12 x 18″

Richard Diebenkorn is perhaps the best known of a group of figurative painters who are associated with the San Francisco Bay area and the colleges and universities where they have been active as teachers. His is already a somewhat historic role stemming from his renunciation of non-objective painting in 1955. He was not the first to make this decision, David Park having done so in 1950, Elmer Bischoff in 1953. But his decision was the more noticeable in that he had already established a considerable place among the abstract expressionist painters of the West Coast. As has been the case so frequently, the relationship of figuration to abstraction has been oversimplified as an either/or matter, as though the artist's responses to experience were of two different kinds. Diebenkorn's abstract pictures remain among the best of their kind even today, full of the instinctual flow of color and movement of brush that can create the kind of pictograph which is the exact equivalent of the painter's subjective experience. Regarded by some as an artistic renegade at the time, Diebenkorn has demonstrated his belief in figuration with skill and distinction, fully confirming his reputation and defining his role as a catalyst among a number of California artists.

Among the painters whose work resembles his, Diebenkorn has maintained a distinctive individuality. His work has been until recently characterized by taut, assertive composition, an intense California color, a rich substantiality of pigment. There is a mood of detachment in his pictures, whether they are concerned with figures in interiors or figures in landscapes, pure landscapes or even empty rooms. The figures seem to be sunk in a kind of languor, drenched in the hot light and immobile on the grid of space where they are placed. It has been noted before that the atmosphere of Diebenkorn's world is strikingly similar to that of Edward Hopper's in its stillness, fixity, and disengagement. Yet, with this similarity there is combined something of the bright, lyric hedonism most readily associated in our time with Matisse.

In any case, the artist has grown in his ability to use and reuse, consciously and unconsciously, varying affinities, and withal to expand his own capacity to see. In his newest work there is some of this new mastery. The statement is less assertive than before. There has been a loosening and easing of the composition and the color. The picture plane seems less densely organized, with a lighter, more graceful placement of color suggesting perhaps a Mediterranean maturity after the more youthful thrust and intensity of Southern California.

Biographical Note

Born, Portland, Oregon, 1922

Education
1940–1943, Stanford University; 1946, California School of Fine Arts; 1950, University of New Mexico, M.F.A.

Teaching Positions
1947–1948, California School of Fine Arts; 1952–1953, University of Illinois; 1955–1957, California College of Arts and Crafts; 1958–1966, San Francisco Art Institute; 1966 to present, University of California at Los Angeles

One-man Exhibitions
1948, 1960, California Palace of the Legion of Honor, San Francisco, California; 1951, University of New Mexico, Albuquerque, New Mexico; 1952, 1953, Paul Kantor Gallery, Los Angeles, California; 1954, San Francisco Museum, San Francisco, California; 1954, Allan Frumkin Gallery, Chicago, Illinois; 1956, 1958, 1963, Poindexter Gallery, New York; 1957, Swetzoff Gallery, Boston, Massachusetts; 1960, Pasadena Art Museum, Pasadena, California; 1961, Phillips Collection, Washington, D.C.; 1962, National Institute of Arts and Letters, New York; 1963, M. H. De Young Memorial Museum, San Francisco, California; 1964, Waddington Galleries, London, England; 1964, Washington Gallery of Modern Art, Washington, D.C.; 1965, The Jewish Museum, New York; 1965, Pavilion Gallery, Newport Beach, California; 1967, Stanford University, Palo Alto, California; 1968, Peale House, Pennsylvania Academy of the Fine Arts, Philadelphia, Pennsylvania

Honors and Awards
1946, Albert Bender Grant-in-Aid; 1954, Abraham Rosenberg Fellowship; 1956, Purchase Prize, Second Pacific Coast Biennial; 1962, Tamarind Fellowship

Public Collections
Albright-Knox Art Gallery, Buffalo, New York; Art Gallery of Toronto, Toronto, Canada; Carnegie Museum of Art, Pittsburgh, Pennsylvania; Cincinnati Art Museum, Cincinnati, Ohio; Phillips Collection, Washington, D.C.; Joseph H. Hirshhorn Collection, New York; Los Angeles County Museum, Los Angeles, California; North Carolina Museum of Art, Raleigh, North Carolina; Pasadena Art Museum, Pasadena, California; Oakland Museum, Oakland, California; Readers Digest Association, New York; San Francisco Museum of Art, San Francisco, California; University of Nebraska, Lincoln, Nebraska; University of New Mexico, Albuquerque, New Mexico; Washington University, St. Louis, Missouri; Whitney Museum of American Art, New York; William Rockhill Nelson Gallery of Art, Kansas City, Missouri

Richard Diebenkorn is represented by the Poindexter Gallery, New York

Recollections of a Visit to Leningrad 1965 oil on canvas 73 x 84″

Selected Bibliography

Periodicals

Alloway, Lawrence. "London Chronicle." *Art International*, 2:33–36, Dec 1958–Jan 1959

Architecture and Engineering, 197:5, April 1954, "Abraham Rosenberg Fellowship in Art Awarded to Diebenkorn"

Artforum, 1:23, 25–28, April 1963, "Diebenkorn, Woelffer, Mullican: A Discussion"

Art News, 51:61, Nov 1952, "Exhibition at Paul Kantor Gallery"

——, 53:47, May 1954, "Exhibition of Drawings and Paintings at the Paul Kantor Gallery"

——, 55:51, March 1956, "Exhibition at Poindexter Gallery"

——, 57:13, March 1958, "Exhibition at Poindexter Gallery"

——, 59:13, March 1961, "Exhibition at Poindexter Gallery"

——, 62:54, Dec 1963, "Exhibition at Poindexter Gallery"

——, 64:54, March 1965, "Exhibition at The Jewish Museum"

Arts, 30:56, March 1956, "Exhibition at Poindexter Gallery"

——, 32:56, March 1958, "Recent Figurative Paintings in Exhibition at Poindexter Gallery"

——, 33:48, Dec 1958, "This Year's Whitney Annual"

——, 35:50, Dec 1960, "Park, Bischoff, Diebenkorn at Staempfli"

Arts and Architecture, 75:29, March 1958, "Flight into Reality in the Poindexter Gallery"

Ashbery, John. "Paris Notes." *Art International*, 7:76–78, June 1963

Ashton, Dore. "An Eastern View of the San Francisco School." *Evergreen Review*, 2:148–59, 1957

——. "Flight into Reality at the Poindexter." *Arts and Architecture*, 78:29, May 1958

——. "New York Report." *Kunstwerk*, 17:27, Jan 1964

——. "Young Painters in Rome." *Arts Digest*, 29:5, June 1955

Baigell, M. "American Abstract Expressionism and Hard Edge, Some Comparisons." *Studio*, 171:12, Jan 1966

Baker, Richard B. "California Artist at Staempfli." *Art News*, 59:15, Dec 1960

——. "Notes on the Formation of my Collection." *Art International*, 5:40–47, Sept 20, 1961

Chipp, H. B. "Diebenkorn Paints a Picture; Woman by the Ocean." *Art News*, 56:44–47, May 1957

——. "Retrospective Assembled by Pasadena Art Museum." *Art News*, 59:54, Feb 1961

Colt, Priscilla. "Remarks on the Figure and Lester Johnson." *Art International*, 7:64–67, Jan 1964

Coplans, John. "Circle of Styles on the West Coast." *Art in America*, 52:26, June 1964

——. "Notes from San Francisco." *Art International*, 7:73–74, May 1963

Greenburg, Clement. "After Abstract Expressionism." *Art International*, 6:24–32, Oct 1962

Grey, D. "Tamarind Workshop." *Art in America*, 51:73–74, Oct 1963

Kaufman, B. "New Kind of Humanism." *Commonweal*, 64:310–11, June 16, 1961

——. "Diebenkorn." *Commonweal*, 81:755–56, March 5, 1965

Kessler, C. S. "Los Angeles, the Seasonal Tide." *Arts*, 35:19, Nov 1960

Kramer, Hilton. "Latest Thing in Pittsburgh." *Arts*, 36:26, Jan 1962

——. "Pure and Impure Diebenkorn." *Arts*, 38:46–53, Dec 1963 (reply: L. Rapp. 38:6, Feb 1964)

Kunstwerk, 43:67, Nov 4, 1957, "Sweeping Patterns from California Fields"

Lanes, J. "Brief Treatise on Surplus Values: or, The Man Who Wasn't There: Exhibition Called New Images of Man at the Modern." *Arts*, 34:30–31, Nov 1959

Langsner, Jules. "Is There an American Print Revival? Tamarind Workshop." *Art News*, 60:35, Jan 1962

Leider, Philip. "California After the Figure." *Art in America*, 51:99, Oct 1963

——. "Diebenkorn Drawings at Stanford." *Artforum*, 2:41–42, May 1964

Lucie-Smith, E. "London Commentary." *Studio*, 173:39, Jan 1967

Lynton, Norbert. "London Letter." *Art International*, 5:96–97, May 1962

Magloff, J. "De Young Museum Exhibition." *Art News*, 62:52, Jan 1964

Mills, P. "Bay Area Figurative." *Art in America*, 52:44, June 1964

Monte, James. "Richard Diebenkorn, De Young Museum." *Artforum*, 2:43, Nov 1963

Munro, Eleanor C. "Figures to the Fore." *Horizon*, 2:16–24, July 1960

Newsweek, 64:97, Nov 30, 1964, "Ethics of Adversity"

Nordland, Gerald "6 x 5." *Frontier*, 7:23–24, Oct 1956

Oberlin College Bulletin, 16, No. 1:18–23, Fall 1958, "Diebenkorn's Woman by a Large Window"

Preston, Stuart. "Art History's Many Turning Points." *New York Times*, Jan 17, 1965

Raynor, V. "Exhibition at Jewish Museum Gallery." *Arts*, 39:54, March 1965

Rexroth, Kenneth. "Figurative Art Revival." *San Francisco Examiner*, Sept 15, 1963

Rose, Barbara. "New York Letter." *Art International*, 8:52–6, April 1964
Sandler, Irving G. "New York Letter." *Art International*, 4:52–54, May 1961
Schevill, James. "Richard Diebenkorn." *Frontier*, 8:21–22, Jan 1957
Seckler, D. G. "Painting." *Art in America*, 46, No. 4:34, Winter 1958–59
Temko, Allan. "The Flowering of San Francisco." *Horizon*, 1:13–15, Jan 1959
Tillim, Sidney. "Exhibition at the Poindexter Gallery." *Arts*, 35:72, April 1965
Time, 71:64–65, March 17, 1958, "Edging Away from Abstraction"
Van der Marck, Jan. "The Californians." *Art International*, 7:28–31, May 1963
Ventura, A. "Prospect Over the Bay." *Arts*, 37:20, May 1963
———. "San Francisco: the Aloof Community." *Arts*, 39:72, April 1965
Wallis, N. "Exhibition at Waddington Galleries." *Apollo*, 80:324, Oct 1964
Whittet, G. S. "London Commentary." *Studio*, 168:274, Dec 1964

Exhibition Catalogs (arranged chronologically)

Solomon R. Guggenheim Museum, New York, "Younger American Painters," May 12 through July 25, 1954
Oberlin College Allen Memorial Art Museum, "Three Young Americans: Glasco, McCullough, Diebenkorn," April 1955
Oakland Art Museum, "Contemporary Bay Area Figurative Painting," 1957. Text by Paul Mills
Fogg Art Museum, "Modern Painting, Drawing and Sculpture, Collected by Louise and Joseph Pulitzer, Jr.," April 9 through September 15, 1957. Text by Charles Scott Chetham
Museum of Modern Art, New York, "New Images of Man," with statements by the artists, 1959. Text by Peter Selz
The Phillips Collection, Washington, D.C., "Richard Diebenkorn," May 19 through June 26, 1961. Text by Gifford Phillips
Pasadena Art Museum, "Richard Diebenkorn," September 6 through October 6, 1961. Text by Gifford Phillips
Amon Carter Museum, Fort Worth, Texas, "The Artists' Environment: West Coast," 1962. Text by Frederick S. Wight
University of California at Los Angeles, "The Gifford and Joann Phillips Collection," November 4 through December 9, 1962
Washington Gallery of Modern Art, Washington, D.C., "Richard Diebenkorn," November 6 through December 31, 1964. Text by Gerald Nordland

Folding Chair 1966 oil on canvas 51 x 48″

Large Woman   1967   oil on canvas   91 x 82″

Window   1967   oil on canvas   92 x 80″

Some few years ago, in response to the sudden flowering of Pop Art, there were desperate predictions that the movement could come to no good end and that the best one could hope for would be an early reaction, somehow salutary, to the revolution which had been accomplished with such ease. By now, of course, the revolution itself is old and Pop's masters have moved on to their own maturity and complexity.

One might include Frank Gallo among the heirs of the Pop revolution. The inheritance is there in the particularity of the subjects, the evocation of a cocktail culture, and the use of an industrial material, but a second and more searching look will reveal that there are differences of a purely qualitative kind.

First of all, we are reminded that there is a tradition, however slight, for this kind of statement, a tradition which may be more apparent in painting than in sculpture. It includes such semi-satiric commentary as occurred in the early decades of the century in the wire sculptures of Alexander Calder, and today in the work of William King. If it be admitted that Gallo's works are satirical in intent, then it must also be understood that this is the satire of identification and affection. However aptly he has summed up the ridiculous or pathetic aspects of reality, he is certainly not out to destroy by ridicule, but rather to recognize by celebration. No more discerning embodiment of today's adolescent female

Girl on Couch 1967 epoxy resin 48 x 51 x 40″

could be imagined. These slim, boneless creatures are the nymphs of the day, true sirens of the Twentieth Century: bold and unabashed in their nakedness, friendly, accessible, untroubled by intellect, supremely at ease, poised between playfulness and languor. Yet, there are glimpses of still other qualities. In several instances there is something of the hushed poise of those ladies of the Renaissance, the creations of Laurana or Desiderio. And, in the creamy glow of their trance-like state there is the transient reflection of Medardo Rosso. In rarer, off-beat moments of the artist's creative mood there occur portraits in a startling, even macabre style, which employ inserted eyes and teeth, echoing the intensities found in the religious sculpture of Spain and Mexico.

Gallo's handling of the male image is perhaps less striking, less "contemporary," but it is no less effective. *Man in Rocker* and *The Critic* are creatures trapped in self-awareness. They have an introspective, worried look; they are very much the men of our time, but their withdrawn manner, their seeming dejection of spirit have a quality of mood that is intelligent even though melancholy.

Obviously, Gallo's greatest innovation is a technical one, employing epoxy resins to create cast forms of extraordinary lightness and exceptional strength. Although relatively easy to reproduce, these sculptures are hand finished and do not necessarily duplicate one another in color or detail. The relatively short period of time in which the artist has been creating them has seen a development from a simple and generalized form, a shell on which features were merely indicated, to a form of much higher finish, particularized detail, and richer color.

Biographical Note

Born, Toledo, Ohio, 1933

Education
1954, Toledo Museum of Art, BFA; 1955, Cranbrook Academy of Art; 1959, State University of Iowa, MFA

Teaching Positions
1960 to present, Professor of Sculpture, University of Illinois, Urbana, Illinois

One-man Exhibitions
1955, Toledo Museum of Art, Toledo, Ohio; 1963, 1964, 1965, 1966, Gilman Galleries, Chicago, Illinois; 1964, Sherry-Netherland Hotel (Gilman Galleries), New York; 1965, 1967, Graham Gallery, New York; 1966, Felix Landau Gallery, Los Angeles, California; 1966, University of Wisconsin, Madison, Wisconsin

Honors and Awards
1966, John Simon Guggenheim Fellowship; 1967, International Sculpture Symposium, Toronto, Canada

Public Collections
Art Institute of Chicago, Chicago, Illinois; Art Gallery of Toronto, Toronto, Canada; Baltimore Museum of Art, Baltimore, Maryland; Cleveland Museum of Art, Cleveland, Ohio; Colorado State University, Fort Collins, Colorado; Joseph H. Hirshhorn Collection, New York; Kalamazoo Institute of Arts, Kalamazoo, Michigan; Los Angeles County Museum of Art, Los Angeles, California; Museo de Bellas Artes, Caracas, Venezuela; Museum of Modern Art, New York; National Gallery of Victoria, Melbourne, Australia; Princeton University, Princeton, New Jersey; Sara Roby Foundation, New York; State University of Iowa, Iowa City, Iowa; University of Wisconsin, Madison, Wisconsin

Frank Gallo is represented by the Gilman Galleries, Chicago, Illinois; the Graham Gallery, New York; and the Felix Landau Gallery, Los Angeles, California

Selected Bibliography

Periodicals

Art in America, 53:61, June 1965, "New Interior Decorators"
———, 54:26–27, July 1966, "New Talent USA"
Art News, 63:21, Dec 1964, "Exhibition at Sherry-Netherland Hotel Gallery"
———, 64:13, Nov 1965, "Exhibition at Graham Gallery"
———, 66, No. 7:14, Nov 1967, "Exhibition at Graham Gallery"
Arts, 40:58, Jan 1966, "Exhibition at Graham Gallery"
———, 42:56, Nov 1967, "Exhibition at Graham Gallery"
Glueck, Grace. "New Work at New York's Graham Gallery." *Art in America*, 53:121, Dec 1965
———, "Trend Toward Trendlessness." *Art in America*, 55:122, Nov–Dec 1967
New York Times, Nov 14, 1965, "Frank Gallo: Simultaneous Identical Shows in Chicago and New York"

Exhibition Catalogs (arranged chronologically)

Gilman Galleries, Chicago, Illinois. "Frank Gallo." October 31 through November 1965
Felix Landau Gallery, Los Angeles, California. "Recent Sculpture by Frank Gallo." December 7 through
    January 9, 1967

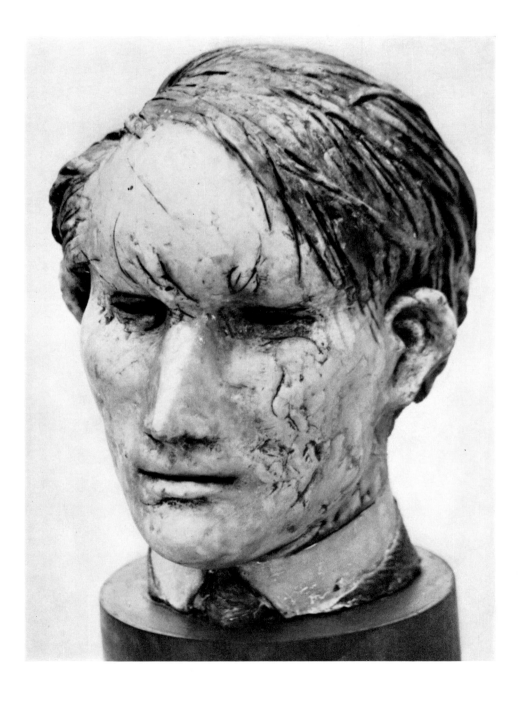

The Critic   1964   epoxy resin   13 x 11 x 13″

Man in Rocker   1965   epoxy resin   40 x 32 x 13″

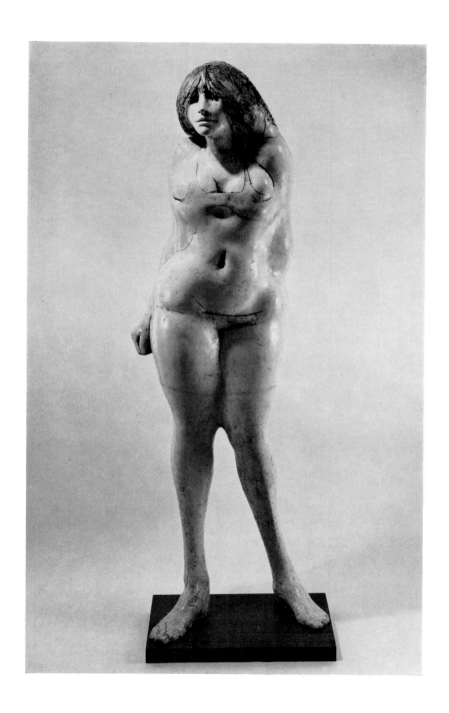

Standing Beach Figure   1966   epoxy resin   64½ x 17 x 11″

Substantial numbers of American artists are working with that big, wide, deep reservoir of American popular art which takes shape in what Americans refer to as the funny papers, the comic books, or the movies, particularly the old movies, gangster movies, campy musicals, routine westerns, or the newer manifestations of the TV screen. This kind of art is obviously related to what is fashionably and now historically known as Pop Art, but it is also a little different. The masters of the Pop movement, Warhol, Rosenquist, and Lichtenstein, have all used these same materials, but with a degree of intellectual sophis-itcation which has removed most of their popular flavor. Only Claes Oldenburg has kept the natural feel of the originals, the quality of happy mockery which is at least half the fun.

In any case, there is still a good deal of this basic folk art in the work of these other artists, none of whom can be called Pop artists in the strictest sense. Red Grooms is probably the purest of them. The ancient cliché about the man and his work being in-separable has never been truer than in the case of Red Grooms. He is his work; to describe him is to run the terrible risk of condescension, to make him and his work seem to be something which need not be taken seriously, to suggest that boys will be boys and that homey, countrified ingenuity is after all charming but of no real account. Such is not the

City of Chicago (detail)   1967   installation of painted wood and paper

City of Chicago (detail)   1967   installation of painted wood and paper

City of Chicago (detail) 1967 installation of painted wood and paper

City of Chicago (detail)   1967   installation of painted wood and paper

Among the American painters of his generation, James McGarrell has always occupied a special place. Although he has been associated with the figurative painters of California, one has only to compare his work with that of Richard Diebenkorn, for instance, to see how different an artist he is. It is true that both men frequently deal with an interior-exterior location and often with an important emphasis placed on figures in that situation. It is also true that both men use color in an overall patterning of the picture plane, but it is still a very different kind of canvas in spite of such similarities.

McGarrell has been called a surrealist, and certainly there is much in his work that suggests the imagery of the unconscious and the irrational. In his pictures there is always a mystery, sometimes declared, sometimes only vaguely defined as a disquieting mingling of forms or an arbitrary interchange of spatial relationships.

Significantly, the irrational element in McGarrell's work is contained within a plausible setting of human artifacts. Within this setting the scrambling of forms and actions and props can be mad enough for the most dedicated devotee of free association, but it is still inside the normal context of experience. Its virtue as a pictorial statement is in its hypothetical character. It challenges one kind of rationality in favor of another by setting up a whole new method of response to the act of seeing and the object seen. It redefines a whole vocabulary of elements : indoors, outdoors, light, dark, air, and water.

The effect upon the observer is frequently that of a performance by a dazzlingly skillful magician, a master of legerdemain. Things happen before your very eyes with such ease and flourish that the conclusion of the act has come and gone before you know it, to be superseded by another feat of fooling the eye. It would appear that McGarrell does not believe in facts as fixed or immovable, that instead he is in a state of constant visual query. What is happening, where, when and why? It is an exhilarating and exhausting exercise in the intellectualization of visual experience. It is a game, a dance, a test, a revelation.

More recently the action of the picture, which is hardly an action at all but a trance-like fixity, is simpler, as in *Rainbow* where two figures simply watch the sky-borne phenomenon. In the recent pictures there has also developed a sudden outburst of color. His *Divers* of 1963 has a specifically Islamic glitter, while, again, *Rainbow* is dominated by a more concentrated color, but one which has the romantic intensity of some of the more enthusiastic members of our Hudson River School, or the spiritual melodrama of Caspar David Friedrich.

Biographical Note

Born, Indianapolis, Indiana, 1930

Education
1949–1953, Indiana University ; Summer, 1953, Skowhegan School of Painting and Sculpture ; 1953–1955, University of California at Los Angeles ; 1955–1956, State Academy of Fine Arts at Stuttgart

Teaching Positions
1956–1959, Reed College, Portland, Oregon ; 1960 to present, Indiana University, Bloomington, Indiana

One-man Exhibitions
1955, 1957, 1958, 1962, Frank Perls Gallery, Beverly Hills, California ; 1958, Joslyn Art Museum, Omaha, Nebraska ; 1958, Portland Art Museum, Portland, Oregon ; 1960, 1961, 1963, 1965, 1967, Allan Frumkin Gallery, Chicago, Illinois ; 1965, Galatea-Galleria d'Arte Contemporanea, Turin, Italy ; 1967, Il Torcoliere-Galeria e Stamperia d'Arte, Rome, Italy ; 1967, Galerie Claude Bernard, Paris, France

Honors and Awards
1955, Fulbright Award ; 1962, Tamarind Fellowship ; 1962, 1963, Ford Foundation Purchase Prize ; 1963, Award and Citation from National Institute of Arts and Letters ; 1964, American Federation of Arts Grant for "Artists-in-Residence in Museums" ; 1964, 1965, John Simon Guggenheim Foundation Fellowship ; 1967, National Foundation on the Arts and Humanities—Sabbatical Grant for Artists Who Teach

Public Collections
Art Institute of Chicago, Chicago, Illinois ; Baltimore Museum of Art, Baltimore, Maryland ; Museum of Modern Art, New York ; National Gallery of Art, Washington, D.C. ; Pennsylvania Academy of the Fine Arts, Philadelphia, Pennsylvania ; Portland Museum of Art, Portland, Oregon ; San Francisco Art Institute, San Francisco, California ; Santa Barbara Art Museum, Santa Barbara, California ; Indiana University, Bloomington, Indiana ; University of Nebraska, Lincoln, Nebraska ; University of Oregon, Eugene, Oregon

James McGarrell is represented by the Allan Frumkin Gallery, New York

Selected Bibliography

Periodicals

Apuleo, Vito. "Allusions and Symbols of a World in Crisis, McGarrell's Lithographs Give Dramatic Expression to a State of Unease." La Voce Repubblicana, Rome, Feb. 24, 1967

Art in America, 52, No. 4:45, August 1964, "Fifty-six Painters and Sculptors"

——, 48, No. 1:28, Spring 1960, "New Talent USA: Painting"

Art News, 60:12, October 1961, "Exhibition at Frumkin Gallery"

——, 63:10, March 1964, "Exhibition at Frumkin Gallery"

——, 65:15, Jan 1967, "Exhibition at Frumkin Gallery"

——, 54:18, Dec 1955, "Los Angeles: Images of Umbrellas; First One-Man Show, Perls Gallery"

Arts, 36:42, Oct 1961, "Exhibition at Frumkin Gallery"

——, 38:34, March 1964, "Exhibition at Frumkin Gallery"

Block, Amanda. "McGarrell's Star Shines at Talbot." *Indianapolis Indiana News*, Oct 3, 1966

Bouret, Jean. "Sept jours avec la peinture." *Les Lettres Françaises*, Paris, Nov 1967

Canaday, John. "Art: From King Gustaf's Chinoiserie." *New York Times*, Jan 7, 1967

Del Guercio, Antonio. "Personaggio e ambiente in McGarrell." *Rinascita*, Rome, Feb 19, 1966

Gruen, John. "57th Street Environs." *New York World Journal Tribune*, Dec 23, 1966

Indianapolis Indiana News, Sept 29, 1966, "McGarrell One-man Show to Open Sunday at Talbot"

——, Nov 24, 1966, "$7,500 Grant Given"

Kosloff, Max. "McGarrell." *Art International*, viii:3, April 1964

Langsner, Jules. "Show in Los Angeles." *Art News*, 61:22, Dec 1962

Micacchi, Dario. "Il 'Paradiso Perduto' de James McGarrell." *L'Unita*, Milan, Feb 9, 1966

Momento Sera, Rome, Feb 12–13, 1966, "McGarrell al Fante di Spade"

Moses, Paul. "The Essence of Reality." *Chicago Daily News*, March 20, 1965

Nordland, G. "Report from Los Angeles." *Arts*, 37:55, Dec 1962

Tillim, Sidney. "Fifty California Artists at the Whitney Museum." *Arts*, 37:40, Dec 1962

Exhibition Catalogs (arranged chronologically)

Frank Perls Gallery, "James McGarrell," October 24 through November 24, 1962

Allan Frumkin Gallery, "The Graphic Works of James McGarrell," 1963

Allan Frumkin Gallery, "Recent Paintings By James McGarrell," February 4 through February 29, 1965

Galatea-Galleria d'Arte Contemporanea, Turin, Italy, "McGarrell," October 15 through November 8, 1965. Text by Luigi Carluccio

Il Torcoliere-Galleria e Stamperia d'Arte, Rome, Italy, "James McGarrell," February 10 through February 28, 1967. Text by Enrico Crispolti

Galerie Claude Bernard, Paris, France, "McGarrell," November 1967. Text by Giovanni Testori

Rainbow   1967   oil on canvas   92 x 77″

Divers 1963 oil on canvas 94 x 81″

Double Corner 1966 oil on canvas 72 x 60″

In twentieth century American art there is a recurrent phenomenon that appears to have its origins in the state of crisis and revolution, which has been so large a part of the art history of the period. In the several instances that spring to mind most easily, there is, to begin with, an individual of natural talent, sometimes native, sometimes not, who begins his career conventionally, probably traditionally, and not uncommonly with a degree of public success. Somewhere in the history of this individual (it usually occurs when the first contact with Europe reveals the cumulative revolutions of Impressionism, Cubism, Fauvism, and Surrealism) a point is reached where the inherited background, the conventional vision, must be renounced for the sake of an entirely new way of seeing. One thinks at once of Americans like Marsden Hartley, Alfred Maurer, and Joseph Stella, whose careers and achievements are scarred by this kind of disruption. In some instances the resolution is tragic, in others it is triumphant, even if in part acquiescent.

Since World War II the phenomenon has continued, but with a difference. Now it is not so much a coming to terms with Europe and Paris, as with a purely native crisis, and less in matters of style than in matters of sensibility. In these post-war years American art has achieved an unprecedented maturity. In instance after instance, the hesistant obedience to standards external to our own experience has consumed a large part of the working span of numerous talented artists. In this generation one thinks of such painters as Jackson Pollock and Philip Guston and of such sculptors as Reuben Nakian.

Within a period of thirty years, beginning at about the age of forty, Nakian has emerged as one of the major artists of our time. What was left behind—an apprenticeship with Paul Manship, an association with Gaston Lachaise, a long conformance to the pedestrian average of the period—seems almost the work of another man. It is perhaps impossible to say what exactly caused the change. Probably it was the feeling in the air— the example of other artists, painters, sculptors, printmakers, poets, and critics—who were breaking out of the patterns of the past at the same time.

In any case, the emergence of a truly splendid artist took place in the exhibitions at the Egan Gallery in 1949 and during the fifties. These were exhibitions filled with a light and movement and, even more, a sensuousness of statement which had certainly not been present in such powerful form in American sculpture since the death of Lachaise in 1935. This quality is particularly apparent in the long series of terra cotta plaques inscribed with the varying images of *Europa and the Bull*, the *Rape of Lucrece*, the *Duchess of Alba*. The completely intuitive balance of material and idea, the sensory appeal of the lovely earth-brown slabs of clay, makes these works unique in American art. There is little with which to compare them. They have the freshness of prehistoric pinched clay figurines, and yet they are different and their difference is in their contemporaneity. These earliest Nakians— the plasters, the terra cottas—and all the subsequent works in steel and bronze have been accompanied by a veritable torrent of drawings. One gets the impression of an impulse so urgent that no single page is expected to contain more than a minute part of the whole. They could, indeed, constitute a kind of hand-drawn motion picture of astounding fluidity.

Between 1955 and 1961 Nakian was involved with a series of large scale works in sheet steel which were, and still are, among the most adventurous and challenging of his works. In this series, which includes the *Rape of Lucrece* now at the Museum of Modern Art, the *Duchess of Alba* belonging to the Los Angeles County Museum, the *Mars and Venus* now at the Albright-Knox Art Gallery, and the commissioned work for the facade of the Loeb Student Center at New York University, the reinterpretation of set-piece themes achieves new heights of dramatic invention. These works, all of which except the last were shown together at the VI Bienal at São Paulo in 1961, seem to have marked the completion of a specific phase of development, for in the years since the artist's thinking has taken a very different form, more personal and less obviously related to anyone else in his ambience.

In 1960 Nakian began the first of the monumental works which have preoccupied him to the present. These include his *Hecuba*, which in its present form seems to be the only surviving vestige of an earlier embodiment of the Trojan theme : a much larger treatment of the subject, *Hecuba on the Burning Walls of Troy*, which was completed, exhibited at the Egan Gallery, and destroyed by the artist in 1954. This was also the fate of a *Maja*, completed in 1963 and destroyed in 1965. Favorite themes are not only repeated but are also subject to a constant reworking. As his conception changes and new embodiments take shape, the older versions must make way by their actual destruction. With each theme the idea is examined over and over again, each variation revealing some new aspect, some fresh overtone of mood or movement.

The *Judgment of Paris* was completed in the fourth of its component figures, that of Minerva, in 1966. This is the drama of human choice played on a stage and a scale of gigantic proportions. Frank O'Hara has referred to it as "Fatalistic yet bawdy ritual." It is a work which, in its expanded scale and in its creation of a dramatic relationship in an open

The Dance of Death:

Herod   1966/67   plaster for bronze   102 x 76 x 63″
Herodias   1966/67   plaster for bronze   105 x 57 x 39″
Salomé   1966/67   plaster for bronze   96 x 72 x 42″

ensemble of figures, is very much a part of the contemporary effort to make art of environment.

Following these works are three of Nakian's most unusual conceptions: the *Goddess of the Golden Thighs*, the *Hiroshima*, and the recently completed *Dance of Death*, which is the latest embodiment of his long involvement with the study of Salomé. These are Nakian's largest works to date and their actual scale is not the sole attribute of their bigness. The *Goddess of the Golden Thighs* is a consummation of Europa, Leda, Olympia, Venus, Juno, Minerva, Salomé, and Herodias. This is indeed the great female deity who has lived in art from the remotest times, the splendidly and generously erotic earth mother.

This note in Nakian's work is perhaps the single most important element in setting him apart from his contemporaries. In his drawings and sculpture there is a continuous celebration of the natural, healthy play of the erotic instinct. It is, of course, justified by the artist's chosen range of subjects, almost all of which derive from classic mythology or biblical history, but it is obvious enough that Nakian is no latter-day classical revivalist and that his sublimation of the traditionally idealized material has taken a thoroughly Romantic direction. This celebration utilizes the full vocabulary of modern expressionism. Leda and Europa have nothing of the victim about them; rather, they appear to be joyous participants in rites of self-realization. There is something truly pre-Christian about Nakian's passion for these themes.

Preceding *The Dance of Death*, only by reason of its earlier completion, is a work which might well be considered Nakian's most remarkable creative feat, his *Hiroshima* of 1965–66. There is nothing here as banal as the mushroom cloud. Instead, there is a great boiling column of energy, a dense amalgam of light and dark, solid and void, contracting and expanding in an almost sensate purity. In one of his rare departures from traditional figuration, he has made real the most characteristic achievement of our time, a pure abstraction.

Finally comes the realization of another project which appears to have figured in Nakian's thinking for at least twenty years. Again, in the manner of the *Judgment of Paris*, it is an ensemble of forces, Salomé, Herod and Herodias, whom Nakian presents to us under the title of *The Dance of Death*. Here there is a more contorted, tortured relationship than the menhir-like solemnity of the *Judgment of Paris*; it is more closely related to the convoluted form of *Hiroshima*. The innate drama of human relationships attains the same intensity, the same exaltation of form, and affirms Nakian's place among the major sculptors of our time.

Biographical Note

Born, College Point, Long Island, New York, 1897

Education
1912, Art Students League, New York (one month); 1915, Life drawing classes, Independent Art School, New York; 1915, Studied clay sculpture, Beaux-Arts Institute, New York; 1916, Studied with Paul Manship and Gaston Lachaise

Teaching Positions
1946–1951, Newark School of Fine and Industrial Arts, Newark, New Jersey; 1952–1954, Pratt Institute, Brooklyn

Exhibitions
1920–1922, *Jack Rabbit* at Salons of America, Anderson Galleries, New York; 1923, Six carved animals

in the "Exhibition of Paintings by John Dos Passos and Adelaide J. Lawson and Sculpture by Reuben Nakian," Whitney Studio Club, New York; 1923, Included in Salons of America, Anderson Galleries; 1926, First one-man exhibition, Whitney Studio Club, New York; 1926, In the "Exhibition of Tri-National Art: British, French, American," Wildenstein Galleries, New York; 1930, One-man exhibition, seven sculptures of seals, Downtown Gallery, New York; 1930, Six works included in "33 Moderns," Grand Central Galleries, New York; 1930, Four works included in "46 Painters and Sculptors under 35 Years of Age," Museum of Modern Art, New York; 1933, One-man exhibition, "Portraits of 10 Artists," Downtown Gallery, New York; 1933, Included in the "International Exhibition of Sculpture," Philadelphia Museum of Art; 1933, In the "First Biennial Exhibition of Contemporary American Sculpture, Watercolors and Prints," Whitney Museum of American Art, New York; 1934, *Babe Ruth*, one-work exhibition, Downtown Gallery, New York; 1935, "Portrait Heads of Officials of the Present Administration," one-man exhibition, Corcoran Gallery of Art, Washington, D.C., also shown at Downtown Gallery, New York; 1938, In "Trois Siècles d'Art aux Etats-Unis," Musée de Jeu de Paume, Paris; 1944, In "Kelekian as the Artist Sees Him," Durand-Ruel Galleries, New York; 1949, "Stone Drawings," exhibited at Egan Gallery, New York; 1950, Terra cottas, one-man exhibition, Egan Gallery, New York; 1952, One-man exhibition, including *Voyage to Crete*, Egan Gallery, New York; 1954, One-man exhibition, including *Venus*, Egan Gallery, New York; 1955, *La Chambre à Coucher de l'Empereur* exhibited, Egan Gallery, New York; 1958, *Rape of Lucrece* included in one-man exhibition, Stewart-Marean Gallery, New York; 1959, *Rape of Lucrece* exhibited on extended loan, Museum of Modern Art, New York; 1960, One-man exhibition of terra cottas, Egan Gallery, New York; 1960, Exhibition of the steels *Mars and Venus* and *Duchess of Alba*, Egan Gallery, New York; 1961, One-man exhibition, U.S. Representation, VI Bienal, São Paulo, Brazil; 1962, *Hecuba, Trojan Woman, Olympia, Voyage to Crete*, exhibited, Egan Gallery, New York; 1962, One-man exhibition, Los Angeles County Museum of Art; 1962, Seven works included in "Continuity and Change," Wadsworth Atheneum, Hartford, Connecticut; 1962, Eight works in "Modern Sculpture from the Joseph H. Hirshhorn Collection," Solomon R. Guggenheim Museum, New York; 1963, One-man exhibition, Washington Gallery of Modern Art, Washington, D.C.; 1963, Included in "Sculpture: Open-Air Exhibition of Contemporary British and American Works," Battersea Park, London; 1964, *Mars and Venus* exhibited, U.S. Pavilion, New York World's Fair; 1964, One-man exhibitions, Egan Gallery, New York; 1964, Included in "International Exhibition of Paintings and Sculpture," Carnegie Institute, Pittsburgh, Pennsylvania; 1965, *La Chambre à Coucher de l'Empereur*, bronze, exhibited at White House Festival of the Arts, Washington, D.C.; 1965, One-man exhibition, including terra cottas, *Judgment of Paris* and *Goddess of the Golden Thighs*, Egan Gallery, New York; 1965, Included in "Actitudas Plasticas," University of Mexico, Mexico City; 1965, Included in "Etats-Unis: Sculptures du XXe Siècle," Musée Rodin, Paris, and West Germany; 1965, In "Critics' Choice: Art Since World War II," Providence, Rhode Island Art Club; 1965, In "Roots of Abstract Art in America," National Collection of Fine Arts, Smithsonian Institution, Washington, D.C.; 1966, Retrospective exhibition, Museum of Modern Art, New York; 1966, Included in "Art of the United States: 1670–1966," Whitney Museum of American Art, New York; 1967, *The Dance of Death* exhibition, Egan Gallery, New York; 1967, One-man exhibition, Felix Landau Gallery, Los Angeles; 1967–1968, "Reuben Nakian: Small Bronzes, Terra Cottas and Drawings," circulating exhibition, Museum of Modern Art, New York; 1967, Included in "Sculpture: a Generation of Innovation," Art Institute of Chicago; 1967, In "American Sculpture of the Sixties," Los Angeles County Museum of Art and Philadelphia Museum of Art, which exhibited *Goddess of the Golden Thighs*, bronze, on extended loan.

Honors and Awards
1919, Fellowship to Louis Comfort Tiffany Foundation Farm, Oyster Bay, New York; 1920–1928, Award of monthly stipend from Gertrude Vanderbilt Whitney; 1931, Guggenheim Fellowship; 1958, Grant, Ford Foundation; 1960, Won New York University competition for facade sculpture, Loeb Student Center, Washington Square, New York; 1966, Received commission for Reynolds Aluminum Award Sculpture; 1967, Awarded Gold Medal for Excellence, Philadelphia College of Art

Public Collections
Albright-Knox Art Gallery, Buffalo, New York; Art Institute of Chicago, Chicago, Illinois; Joseph H. Hirshhorn Collection, New York; Los Angeles County Museum of Art, Los Angeles, California; Museum of Modern Art, New York; New York State Theatre, Lincoln Center for the Performing Arts, New York; University of Nebraska, Lincoln, Nebraska; Whitney Museum of American Art, New York

Reuben Nakian is represented by the Egan Gallery, New York; the Felix Landau Gallery, Los Angeles, California; the Donald Morris Gallery, Detroit, Michigan; and the B.C. Holland Gallery, Chicago, Illinois

Selected Bibliography

Books

Contemporary Sculpture : Arts Yearbook 8. New York, Art Digest, 1965
Goodrich, Lloyd and Baur, John I. H. *American Art of Our Century*. New York, Praeger, 1961
Hunter, Sam. *New Art Around the World*. New York, Abrams, 1966
Jaffee, Cynthia. "Nakian." Thesis, New York, Columbia University, 1967
Larkin, Oliver W. *Art and Life in America*. New York, Holt, Rhinehart and Winston, 1964
O'Hara, Frank. *In Memory of My Feelings*. New York, Museum of Modern Art, 1967
————. *Nakian*. New York, Doubleday, 1966
Rose, Barbara. *American Art Since 1900*. New York, Praeger, 1967
Tuchman, Maurice. *American Sculpture of the Sixties*. Los Angeles, Los Angeles County Museum of Art, 1967

Periodicals

Adlow, Dorothy. "Our Daring Sculptors." *Christian Science Monitor*, Sept 2, 1961, p. 10
Ahlander, Leslie. "Two Events of Major Importance." *Washington Post*, Washington, D.C., Jan 13, 1963, G8
America Illustrated, U.S.I.A., 132:1–3, 1967, "Nakian"
Arnason, H. Harvard. "Nakian." *Art International*, 7:36–43, April 1963
Art Digest, 5:14, Nov 15, 1930, "Nakian's Seals"
————, 7:6, Oct 15, 1932, "Nakian's *'Pop' Hart* is Praised by Critics"
————, 7:16, March 1, 1933, "Art Personalities"
————, 8:23, Feb 15, 1934, "*Babe Ruth* by Nakian"
Art News, 61:25, 56, Jan 1963, "Nakian in the Capital"
————, 62:40, Nov 1963, "Entering Public Domain : New York"
The Arts, 5:427, June 1923, "The Exhibitions : Salons of America"
Ashbery, John. "Reviews and Previews : Nakian." *Art News*, 66:16, Jan 1968
Ashton, Dore. "Art : Nakian's Sculpture." *New York Times*, Nov 14, 1958, p. 30
————. "Exhibition at the Egan Gallery." *Studio International*, 169:94, Feb 1965
————. "Recent Sculptures at the Charles Egan Gallery." *Studio International*, 164:8, July 1962
Breuning, Margaret. "Reuben Nakian Mythological Themes." *Art Digest*, 23:17, May 15, 1949
————. "Nakian's Modern Mythology." *Art Digest*, 24:18, April 15, 1950
Burrows, Carlyle. "Nakian : Somber Images." *New York Herald Tribune*, March 18, 1962
Campbell, Lawrence. "Reuben Nakian." *Art News*, 53:56, April 1954
Conant, Howard. "New York University Collection : Nakian." *Art Journal*, 21:1, 22, Fall 1961
De Kooning, Elaine. "Exhibition of Terra-Cotta Plaques at Egan." *Art News*, 48:42–43, May 1949
Dial, 72:464, May 1922, "*Jack Rabbit* : Reuben Nakian"
Dulac, Margarita. "In the Galleries : Nakian." *Arts*, 40:51, Sept 1966
Getlein, Frank. "Art and Artists : Reuben Nakian Show at Gallery of Modern Art Highly Significant." *Washington Star*, Washington, D.C., Jan 13, 1963, C13
Goldwater, Robert. "Reuben Nakian." *Quadrum*, 11:95–102, 1961
Goodrich, Lloyd. "November Exhibitions : Julia Kelly and Reuben Nakian." *The Arts*, 17:121–22, Nov 1930
Gustaitis, Rasa. "New Deal's Busy Sculptor Back in Town." *Washington Post*, Washington, D.C., Dec 30, 1962, B3
Hess, Thomas B. "L'Apres-Midi d'Un Faune : Drawings by Reuben Nakian." *Location*, 1:43–54, Summer 1964
————. "In Praise of Reason." *Art News*, 65:22–25, Summer 1966
————. "Introducing the Steel Sculpture of Reuben Nakian." *Art News*, 57:36–39, 65–66, Nov 1958
————. "November Contrasts." *Art News*, 63:30, 65, Nov 1964
————. "Reuben Nakian." *Ararat*, 4:14–28, Autumn 1963
————. "Today's Artists : Nakian." *Portfolio and Art News Annual*, 4:84–99+, 1961
————. "U.S. Sculpture : Some Recent Directions." *Portfolio and Art News Annual*, 1:112–27+, 1959
Hoene, Anne. "In the Galleries : Reuben Nakian." *Arts*, 40:57–58, Nov 1965
Jewell, Edward Alden. "Assyria and Plug Hats." *New York Times*, March 5, 1933, IX:8
Judd, Donald. "Exhibition at the Egan Gallery." 35:52, Jan 1961

Kozloff, Max. "Art Exhibition at Egan Gallery." *Nation*, 194:320, April 7, 1962
——. "New York Letter: Nakian." *Art International*, 6:82, May 1962
Krasne, Belle. "10 Artists in the Margin." *Design Quarterly*, 30:14–15, 1954
Kramer, Hilton. "Month in Review: Nakian." *Arts*, 33:48–50, Jan 1959
Kuh, Katharine. "Nakian." *America Illustrated*, U.S.I.A., 86:61, 1966
——. "Portraits in Paganism." *Saturday Review*, 48:28–29, July 31, 1965
Lippard, Lucy. "New York Letter: Nakian." *Art International*, 9:42, Nov 1965
——. "Not 'Boring,' But Richly Sensual." *New York Times*, June 26, 1966, II:21
Location, 1:8–15, Spring 1963, "Reuben Nakian: Studio, Drawings, Sculpture." Photographs by Thor Bostrom
McBride, Henry. "*Babe Ruth* in Sculpture." *New York Sun*, Feb 17, 1934, p. 11
Mumford, Lewis. "Portraits in Plaster." *New Yorker*, 11:69–70, May 18, 1935
Munro, Eleanor. "Exploration in Form." *Perspectives*, 16:165, Summer 1956
Nakian, Reuben. "Ego and Eternity: A Dialogue on Late Egyptian Art." *Art News*, 59:28–30, Nov 1960. With Bernard V. Bothmer
——. "Is Today's Artist With or Against the Past." *Art News*, 57:29, June 1958. Interview with Thomas B. Hess
Newsweek, 56:104–5, Nov 21, 1960, "The Crazy Thing To Do"
——, 68:83, July 4, 1966, "I'm on the Satyr's Side"
New York Herald Tribune, June 18, 1933, VI:8, "Museum Receives a Bust of *'Pop' Hart*"
——, April 21, 1935, VI:2, "A Sculptor Looks at the New Deal"
——, July 31, 1960, "NYU Commissions Nakian Sculpture"
New York Times, August 5, 1934, VII:2, "The 'Plastic Appeal' of the New Deal in Sculpture: Reuben Nakian"
——, April 11, 1959, "Sculptor's Concept of *Rape of Lucrece* Put into Museum"
Nordland, Gerald. "An Important Los Angeles Showing." *Frontier*, 13:21–23, June 1962
——. "Southern California Museums." *Kunstwerk*, 16:28, 35, Oct 1962
O'Doherty, Brian. "Art: Mythmaking in the 20th Century." *New York Times*, March 20, 1962, p. 34
Porter, Fairfield. "Art Exhibition at Egan Gallery." *Nation*, 191:512, Dec 24, 1960
——. "Exhibition of Terra-Cottas at Egan Gallery." *Art News*, 51:43, May 1952
Pousette-Dart, Nathaniel. "Reuben Nakian: A Master of Form." *Studio News*, 2:6–7, Feb 1934
Preston, Stuart. "Abstract Romantic." *New York Times*, Nov 20, 1960, II:25
——. "Sculpture by Nakian." *New York Times*, May 8, 1949, II:8
Raynor, Vivien. "Exhibition at the Egan Gallery." *Arts*, 39:64, Dec 1964
Rose, Barbara. "Nakian at the Modern." *Artforum*, 2:18–19, Oct 1966
Rosenberg, Harold. "Art in Orbit." *Art News*, 60:22–26+, Oct 1961
——. "Nakian: Eros and Grief." *Vogue*, 148:64–65+, July 1966
Sandler, Irving. "New York Letter: Nakian." *Art International*, 4:22, Dec 1960
Santiago Nacion, Nov 17, 1966, "Grandeza Abstracta"
Schjeldahl, Peter. "A New Domain." *Village Voice*, 30:11, June 1966
Secunda, Arthur. "Reviews: Los Angeles: Reuben Nakian." *Artforum*, 1:4–5, Aug 1962
Seldis, Henry. "Show Complements Nakian Exuberance." *Los Angeles Times*, May 27, 1962, p. 12
Staten Island Advance, Dec 6, 1938, "'European' Atmosphere on Island Delights Artist"
Time, 59:80, May 12, 1952, "Voyage to Crete"
——, 89:50–51, June 30, 1967, "Demigods from Stamford"
Vogue, 138:90–91, Oct 1961, "Two Great American Artists"
Washington Star, Washington, D.C., April 21, 1934, "President Visits Corcoran Show"
Watson, Forbes. "New York Exhibitions: Nakian." *The Arts*, 10:345–47, Dec 1926
Wedge, Will. "A Ton of Clay to Make Ruth." *New York Sun*, Feb 20, 1934, p. 31

Exhibition Catalogs (arranged chronologically)

New York. Whitney Studio Club. "Exhibition of Paintings by John Dos Passos and Adelaide J. Lawson and Sculpture by Reuben Nakian," 1923
Washington, D.C. Corcoran Gallery of Art. "Nakian: Portrait Heads of Officials of the Present Administration," 1935. Foreword by Henry McBride
Paris. Musée de Jeu de Paume. "Trois Siècles d'Art aux Etats-Unis," 1938. Text by Alfred H. Barr, Jr.
São Paulo. Museu de Arte Moderna, VI Bienal. "Estados Unidos: Nakian," 1961. Text by Thomas B. Hess
Hartford, Connecticut. Wadsworth Atheneum. "Continuity and Change," 1962

Los Angeles. Los Angeles County Museum of Art. "Reuben Nakian: Sculpture and Drawings," 1962. Introduction by Robert Goldwater

New York. Solomon R. Guggenheim Museum. "Modern Sculpture from the Joseph H. Hirshhorn Collection," 1962

London. Battersea Park. "Sculpture: Open-Air Exhibition of Contemporary British and American Works," 1963

Washington, D.C. Washington Gallery of Modern Art. "Nakian," 1963. Text by Thomas B. Hess

New York. Solomon R. Guggenheim Museum. "American Drawings," 1964

Pittsburgh, Pennsylvania. Carnegie Institute. "The 1964 Pittsburgh International Exhibition of Contemporary Painting and Sculpture," 1964

Paris. Musée Rodin. "Etats Unis: Sculptures du XXe Siècle," 1965

Providence, Rhode Island. "Critics' Choice: Art Since World War II," 1965

Washington, D.C. National Collection of Fine Arts, Smithsonian Institution. "Roots of Abstract Art in America 1910–1930," 1965

Austin. University of Texas. "Drawings &," 1966

New York. Public Education Association. "Seven Decades: 1895–1965," 1966

New York. Whitney Museum of American Art. "Art of the United States: 1670–1966," 1966

Richmond. Virginia Museum of Fine Arts. "Visions of Man," 1966

Chicago. Art Institute of Chicago. "Sculpture: A Generation of Innovation," 1967

Los Angeles. Felix Landau Gallery. "Sculpture and Drawings by Reuben Nakian," 1967

New Haven. Yale University. "The Helen W. and Robert M. Benjamin Collection," 1967

Trojan Woman   1960/62   plaster for bronze   109 x 62 x 30″

Olympia 1961 bronze 72 x 74 x 34″

Birth of Venus 1963/66 plaster for bronze 96 x 131 x 66″

Goddess of the Golden Thighs   1964/65   plaster for bronze   108 x 150 x 48″

Judgment of Paris : Venus   1964 /65   plaster for bronze   81 x 88 x 60″

Judgment of Paris : Minerva   1965/66   plaster for bronze   97 x 83 x 50″

Hiroshima   1966   plaster for bronze   111 x 72 x 48″

Few contemporary American painters are so completely a part of the tradition of Impressionist and post-Impressionist painting as Fairfield Porter. But for all his self-announced allegiance to the French tradition, he is inseparably American in the manner of his seeing and in the manner of his doing.

In talking to the artist one learns of his admiration for Corot, Chardin, Courbet, and, obviously enough, Bonnard and Vuillard. The only American painter for whom he expresses any enthusiasm is Copley, this notwithstanding the fact of his published monograph on Thomas Eakins. All of this is easy enough to see in the neutral range of his palette and intimist view of life. Even Copley's unemotional eye and matter-of-fact analysis of forms are not unbelievable sources of inspiration.

However, and here one must recognize that the artist's known predilections are not necessarily the whole story, there would seem to be other connections as well which tell us something more about the artist's achievement. First of all, the light which fills Porter's world has a peculiar blandness, an unequivocal play which penetrates and defines the involved spaces and forms without any commitment to sensory response or emotional reaction. Copley was probably our first important painter to define it, but it operates as well in the work of other American masters, Winslow Homer and Thomas Eakins, and in lesser ways, in the work of William Sidney Mount and George Caleb Bingham. In fact, if one considers the essential difference between American artists of any style or school and their nearest European equivalent, it is usually in precisely this respect that the difference can be seen. The American will restrain or equalize his response, or at least will examine his experience with a more objective eye. If we compare Porter's landscapes and interiors with their obvious French counterparts the difference is immediately discernible. Porter's light is non-sensuous, his color is restrained, his space is in equipoise, never in tension nor even in that state of compositional magnetism which holds a Bonnard together.

In a second sense, Fairfield Porter's pictures are very much a part of a more recent kind of painterly experience. From the beginning of his active career as a painter in the 1940's, he has been closely associated with the development of the whole Abstract Expressionist movement, as friend, associate, and working critic. His perceptions as both painter and writer are based on the sympathies of a mutual point of view. Porter's pictures, however much they have remained within the framework of their subject matter, have always possessed the defining characteristic of pure painterliness. The strongest part of his accomplishment has always been the design of the picture surface, taken as a field for the manipulated interplay of color films. In picture after picture the colors are arranged in mosaic-like patterns, lying flat against each other in an almost fluid juxtaposition. That such a surface filled with Porter's special brand of light can assert the illusion of depth, of wide, deep reaches of space, is an accomplishment of an extraordinary kind. It is perhaps even more remarkable in that it is an accomplishment that fuses tradition with the avant-garde.

Biographical Note

Born, Winnetka, Illinois, 1907

Education
Harvard University, Cambridge, Massachusetts, B.S.; Art Students League of New York, with Boardman Robinson and Thomas Hart Benton

One-man Exhibitions
1939, Community House, Winnetka, Illinois; 1951, Tibor de Nagy Gallery, New York, and annually to the present; 1959, Rhode Island School of Design, Providence, Rhode Island; 1963, University of Alabama, Tuscaloosa, Alabama; 1963, University of Southern California School of Design, Los Angeles, California; 1965, Reed College, Portland, Oregon; 1966, Trinity College, Hartford, Connecticut; 1966, Cleveland Museum of Fine Arts, Cleveland, Ohio; 1967, Kent State University, Kent, Ohio; 1967, Swarthmore College, Swarthmore, Pennsylvania; 1968, Richard Gray Gallery, Chicago, Illinois

Honors and Awards
Longview Foundation Award for criticism of Willem DeKooning's 1959 exhibition published in *The Nation*. (See Bibliography)

Public Collections
Chase Manhattan Bank, New York; Cleveland Museum of Art, Cleveland, Ohio; Corcoran Gallery of Art, Washington, D.C.; Grey Lock Foundation, Williamstown, Massachusetts; Guild Hall, Easthampton, Long Island, New York; Joseph H. Hirshhorn Foundation, New York; Museum of Modern Art, New York; University of Nebraska, Lincoln, Nebraska; University of New Mexico, Albuquerque, New Mexico; Wadsworth Atheneum, Hartford, Connecticut; Whitney Museum of American Art, New York; Woodward Foundation, Washington, D.C.

Fairfield Porter is represented by the Tibor de Nagy Gallery, New York

The Pear Tree   1962   oil on canvas   75 x 60″

Selected Bibliography

Book by Fairfield Porter
Thomas Eakins. New York, Braziller, 1959

Articles by Fairfield Porter (arranged chronologically)
"Evergood Paints a Picture." *Art News*, 51:30–33, Oct 1952
"Vasilieff Paints a Picture." *Art News*, 51:34–37, Oct 1952
"Hartl Paints a Picture." *Art News*, 52:30–33, April 1953
"Tworkov Paints a Picture." *Art News*, 52:30–33, May 1953
"Transatlantic Watercolors." *Art News*, 52:21, June 1953
"Rivers Paints a Picture." *Art News*, 52:56–59, Jan 1954
"Nature of John Marin." *Art News*, 54:24–27, March 1954
"Herman Rose Paints a Picture." *Art News*, 54:38–41, May 1955
"Stankiewicz Makes a Sculpture." *Art News*, 54:36–39, Sept 1955
"Meeting Ground at the Whitney." *Art News*, 55:38–39, May 1956
"Jane Freilicher Paints a Picture." *Art News*, 55:46–49, Sept 1956
"Sargent: An American Problem." *Art News*, 55:38–39, Dec 1956
"George Bellows: Journalists' Artist." *Art News*, 55:32–35, Feb 1957
"David Smith: Steel Into Sculpture." *Art News*, 56:40–43, Sept 1957
"From Inner Space." *Art News*, 56:35, Sept 1957
"American Painters in Words." *Art News*, 57:43, May 1958
"Art Exhibition at the Tibor de Nagy Gallery." *Nation*, 186:428, May 10, 1958
"Homer: American Versus Artist: A Problem in Identities." *Art News*, 57:24–27, Dec 1958
"DeKooning." *Nation*, 188:520, June 6, 1959
"El Greco: Vision of St. John the Evangelist." *Nation*, 189:18, July 4, 1959
"International Interest in American Art." *Nation*, 189:197, Oct 3, 1959
"Reuben Gallery Exhibition." *Nation*, 189:260, Oct 24, 1959
"Sculpture: Two Exhibitions." *Nation*, 189:387, Nov 21, 1959
"Cézanne, Exhibition at Wildenstein." *Nation*, 189:406, Nov 28, 1959
"Art as a History of Drawing." *Art News*, 58:44, Dec 1959
"California and New York Artists." *Nation*, 189:476, Dec 19, 1959
"Color Photographs by Eliot Porter." *Nation*, 190:39, Jan 9, 1960
"Morandi and Vasilieff." *Nation*, 192:67, Jan 21, 1960
"Elmer Bischoff Exhibition and Robert Goodnough." *Nation*, 190:88, Jan, 23, 1960
"Alberto Giacometti." *Nation*, 190:126, Feb 6, 1960
"John Button and Seymour Reminick." *Nation*, 190:154+, Feb 13, 1960
"Hans Arp." *Nation*, 190:234, March 12, 1960
"Piet Mondrian." *Nation*, 190:234, March 12, 1960
"Robert Engman, Jane Freilicher, Paul Georges and Jasper Johns." *Nation*, 190:262, March 19, 1960
"American Artists Exhibitions." *Nation*, 190:301, April 2, 1960
"Claude Monet." *Nation*, 190:301, April 2, 1960
"Degas Exhibition." *Nation*, 190:371, April 23, 1960
"Robert Rauschenberg and Richard Stankiewicz." *Nation*, 190:371, April 23, 1960
"William King." *Nation*, 190:391, April 30, 1960
"Isabel Bishop." *Nation*, 190:458, May 21, 1960
"Constructivist Show." *Nation*, 190:476, May 28, 1960
"Metropolitan Museum, Photography Exhibition." *Nation*, 190:539, June 18, 1960
"Growing Popular Interest in Museums." *Nation*, 191:139, Sept 10, 1960
"John Graham: Painter as Aristocrat." *Art News*, 59:39–41, Oct 1960
"Whitney Museum: Young America Exhibition." *Nation*, 191:215–216, Oct 1, 1960
"Martha Jackson Gallery Exhibition." *Nation*, 191:256, Oct 15, 1960

"Joseph Fiore, Cy Twombly and Ad Reinhardt." *Nation*, 191:356, Nov 5, 1960
"Guggenheim Museum's Third Biennial International Award Exhibition." *Nation*, 191:423, Nov 26, 1960
"James McNeill Whistler and Lovis Corinth." *Nation*, 191:442–43, Dec 3, 1960
"Peter Agostini, Reuben Nakian and the Jefferson Memorial." *Nation*, 191:511, Dec 24, 1960
"Art for Morality's Sake." *Nation*, 191:530, Dec 31, 1960
"Edwin Dickinson, Robert Richenburg and Mark Rothko." *Nation*, 192:175, Feb 25, 1961
"On Alleged Lack of Communication and Moral Commitment in Modern Art." *Nation*, 192:243, March 18, 1961
"Elaine DeKooning and Robert Motherwell." *Nation*, 192:378, April 29, 1961
"National Arts Club Show." *Nation*, 192:446, May 20, 1961
"Whitney Museum, American Painting 1865–1905." *Nation*, 192:506, June 10, 1961
"Class Content in American Abstract Painting." *Art News*, 61:26–28, April 1962
"Education of Jasper Johns." *Art News*, 62:44–45, Feb 1964
"Prendergast Anomaly." *Art News*, 65:36–39, Nov 1966

Periodicals

Art Digest, 27:19, Nov 1952, "Exhibition, Tibor de Nagy Gallery"
———, 28:16, April 1954, "Exhibition of Oils at Tibor de Nagy Gallery"
———, 29:26, Feb 15, 1955, "Exhibition of Paintings at Tibor de Nagy Gallery"
Art in America, 50 No. 1:78–81, May 1962, "Recent Painting USA: The Figure"
———, 55:51, Jan 1967, "Sensibility of the Sixties"
Art News, 51:45, Oct 1952, "Exhibition, de Nagy Gallery"
———, 53:46, April 1954, "Exhibition of Paintings at de Nagy Gallery"
———, 53:38–41, Jan 1955, "Porter Paints a Picture: Portrait of Katherine"
———, 54:49, March 1955, "Exhibition of Paintings at de Nagy Gallery"
———, 55:26, April 1956, "Selecting from the Flow of Spring Shows: Paintings at de Nagy Gallery"
———, 57:13, May 1958, "Exhibition at de Nagy Gallery"
———, 58:13, March 1959, "Exhibition at de Nagy Gallery"
———, 59:12, Nov 1960, "Exhibition at de Nagy Gallery"
———, 60:47, Jan 1962, "Exhibitions for 1961–1962"
———, 61:38, Summer 1962, "U.S. Figure Painting: Continuity and Cliché"
———, 62:13, March 1963, "Exhibition at de Nagy Gallery"
———, 63:36–37, March 1964, "Fairfield Porter: Minimum of Melodrama"
———, 63:46, March 1964, "Towards a Plastic Revolution"
———, 63:11, Feb 1965, "Exhibition at de Nagy Gallery"
———, 64:30–32, Feb 1966, "Art and Knowledge"
———, 65:18, Feb 1967, "Show at de Nagy Gallery"
———, 66:32–33, March 1967, "Immediacy is the Message: Fairfield Porter"
Arts, 30:58, April 1956, "Exhibition at de Nagy Gallery"
———, 32:54, June 1958, "Fifth New York Exhibition"
———, 33:56, March 1959, "Exhibition at de Nagy Gallery"
———, 40:57, April 1966, "Exhibition at de Nagy Gallery"
———, 41:63, April 1967, "Show at de Nagy Gallery"
Grosser, M. "Art Exhibition at the Tibor de Nagy Gallery." *Nation*, 186:428, May 10, 1958
Hess, T. B. "U.S. Painting: Some Recent Directions." *Art News Annual*, 25:84, 1956
Kramer, Hilton. "New York, Season's Gleanings." *Art in America*, 51:134, June 1963
———. "Critics of American Paintings. The First Six Volumes of the Great American Series." *Arts*, 34:29, Oct 1964
Lanes, J. "Fairfield Porter's Recent Work." *Arts*, 38:40–43, April 1964. (Reply with rejoinder: F. Porter, 39:6, Oct 1964)
Nation, 192:220–21, March 11, 1961, "Classic Forms"
Newsweek, 61:62–63, Feb 11, 1963, "Point of Departure"
Rayner, V. "Exhibition at de Nagy Gallery." *Arts*, 39:63, April 1965
Roberts, C. "Lettre de New York." *Aujourd'hui*, 6:60, Sept 1962
Tillim, Sidney. "New Work at the Tibor de Nagy Gallery." *Arts*, 35:45–46, Dec 1960
———. "Exhibition at de Nagy Gallery." *Arts*, 36:38, Feb 1962
———. "Exhibition at de Nagy Gallery." *Arts*, 37:63, March 1963

Time, 83 : 74–75, April 3, 1964, "They Paint ; You Recognize"

Exhibition Catalogs (arranged chronologically)

Wildenstein Gallery, "The Question of the Future," Catalogue of fifty painters selected by an international jury. Text by Alfred Frankfurter. 1960

Tibor de Nagy Gallery, "Fairfield Porter," January 29th through February 16, 1962

Mitchell Gallery, Southern Illinois University, "Fairfield Porter, Paintings," November 1 through November 27, 1964

Tibor de Nagy Gallery, "Fairfield Porter," February 16 through March 6, 1965

Tibor de Nagy Gallery, "Fairfield Porter, Recent Paintings," February 15 through March 5, 1966

Cleveland Museum of Art, "The Genre Art of Fairfield Porter," 1966

Richard Gray Gallery, "Fairfield Porter," March 6 through April 6, 1968

Living Room   1964   oil on canvas   60 x 48"

View of the Harbor   1965   oil on canvas   45 x 45"

Columbus Day   1966   oil on canvas   80 x 80″

(Dimensions are in inches. Height precedes width, precedes depth. *denotes color plate. † not illustrated)

LEONARD BASKIN

SCULPTURE

Small Birdman   1963
Bronze   25½ x 11½ x 14¼"
Lent by Grace Borgenicht Gallery, New York

*Achilles Mourning the Death of Patrocles**   1967
Bronze, 1/5   29 x 32 x 31"
Lent by Grace Borgenicht Gallery, New York

Great Wood Dead Man   1968
Wood   31 x 28½ x 16"
Lent by Grace Borgenicht Gallery, New York

PRINTS AND DRAWINGS

Hanged Man †   1955
Woodcut, unlimited edition   67½ x 20"
Lent by University of Nebraska Art Galleries, Lincoln, Nebraska

Haman †   1956
Woodcut, unlimited edition   47¾ x 23"
Lent by University of Nebraska Art Galleries, Lincoln, Nebraska

Love Me, Love My Dog †   1958
Wood engraving, unlimited edition   7³⁄₁₆ x 6⅛"
Lent by University of Nebraska Art Galleries, Lincoln, Nebraska

Angel of Death †   1959
Woodcut, unlimited edition   61½ x 30½"
Lent by Goodall Gallery, Doane College, Crete, Nebraska

Death Among the Thistles †   1959
Wood engraving, c. 50 impressions   6 x 8"
Lent by University of Nebraska Art Galleries, Lincoln, Nebraska

Eakins: 1895 †   1960
Etching, 38/50   7 x 5"
Lent by University of Nebraska Art Galleries, Lincoln, Nebraska

Menzel †   1963
Etching, artist's proof   18 x 15"
Lent by University of Nebraska Art Galleries, Lincoln, Nebraska

In the Meadow †   1964–65
Etching, 81/100   15 x 8⅝"
Lent by University of Nebraska Art Galleries, Lincoln, Nebraska

Great Man 1964
Ink on paper 87 x 42''
Lent by Grace Borgenicht Gallery, New York

Nightmare 1964
Ink on paper 77 x 42''
Lent by Grace Borgenicht Gallery, New York

BOOKS

Thirteen Poems by Wilfred Owen † 1956 (King 11)
Book of thirteen pages with drawings by Ben Shahn
(Printed by the Meriden Gravure Company)
Portrait of Wilfred Owen engraved by Leonard Baskin from a drawing by Ben Shahn
and printed from the woodblock
Page size: 13½ x 10''
Ludlow Caslon type, Arnold unbleached paper, Half Oasis Niger with paper sides,
in slipcase
400 copies, printed by the Gehenna Press, Northampton, Massachusetts, 1956
Lent by University of Nebraska Art Galleries, Lincoln, Nebraska

The Seven Deadly Sins, † poems by Antony Hecht 1958 (King 19)
Book of ten pages. Wood engravings by Leonard Baskin
Page size: 8 x 8''
Perpetua type, Mokuroku paper, Blue paper wrappers with title label
300 copies, printed by the Gehenna Press, Northampton, Massachusetts, 1958
Lent by University of Nebraska Art Galleries, Lincoln, Nebraska

Homage to Redon † 1959 (King 22)
Book of twenty-four pages. Ten portraits by Leonard Baskin cut and engraved on
wood by George Lockwood, printed from the blocks in black and white and color,
under the artist's supervision, on a variety of Japanese handmade papers
With Redon's essay on Bresdin Lithography and the Nature of Black translated by
Hyman Swetzoff
Page size: 11¼ x 9¼''
Caslon type, Millbourne Book Laid paper, gray boards with Niger Morocco spine,
in slipcase
150 copies, printed by the Gehenna Press, Northampton, Massachusetts, 1959
Lent by University of Nebraska Art Galleries, Lincoln, Nebraska

Auguries of Innocence, † William Blake 1959 (King 24)
Book of eight pages. Eight wood engravings by Leonard Baskin
Page size: 9¼ x 5¾''
Monotype Bembo, Amalfi paper
250 copies, printed by the Gehenna Press, Northampton, Massachusetts, 1959
Lent by University of Nebraska Art Galleries, Lincoln, Nebraska

Note: King numbers given for books refer to the bibliography of Gehenna Press publications by
Dorothy King.

BYRON BURFORD

Explorers' Dinner, No. 2 1966
Oil on canvas   57¾ x 56¾"
Lent by Babcock Galleries, New York

*Homage to Clyde** 1966
Oil on canvas   60 x 60"
Lent by Mrs. Mary Cowell Ross, New York

Mrs. Corsey with Butterflies 1967
Oil and plastic on canvas   100 x 81"
Lent by Babcock Galleries, New York

Jack Earl and Friends 1967
Oil and serigraph on canvas   80" diameter
Lent by Babcock Galleries, New York

ROBERT CREMEAN

The Anatomy Lesson, No. 4 1965
Laminated wood, metal   53 x 66 x 30"
Lent by Esther and Robert Robles, Los Angeles, California

Studies for a Self-Portrait and a Self-Portrait 1966
Wood, oil, graphite   80 x 60" closed ; 80 x 120" open
Lent anonymously

Sibyl 1967
Laminated wood   44¼ x 36 x 24"
Lent by Felix Landau Gallery, Los Angeles, California

The Fourteen Stations of the Cross† 1966–67
Suite of fourteen three-color lithographs   paper size : 22 x 15"
Copy No. 2 of artist's edition, Tamarind Nos. 1879–1892
Lent by Felix Landau Gallery, Los Angeles, California

EDWIN DICKINSON

An Anniversary 1921
Oil on canvas   72 x 60"
Lent by Albright-Knox Art Gallery, Buffalo, New York
Gift of Mr. and Mrs. Ansley W. Sawyer

The Cello Player 1924–26
Oil on canvas   60 x 48¼"
Lent by Sara Roby Foundation, New York

Girl on Tennis Court   1926
Oil on panel   36 x 30"
Lent by Nebraska Art Association, Lincoln, Nebraska. Gift of Mrs. A. B. Sheldon

Woodland Scene   1929–35
Oil on canvas   71⅜ x 68½"
Lent by Andrew Dickson White Museum of Art, Cornell University, Ithaca, New York. Given by Esther Hoyt Sawyer in memory of William Ballard Hoyt

Cottage Porch, Peaked Hill   1932
Oil on canvas   26⅛ x 30⅛"
Lent by Museum of Modern Art, New York. Grace Rainey Rogers Fund

Stranded Brig   1934
Oil on canvas   40 x 50"
Lent by Museum of Fine Arts, Springfield, Massachusetts

Rock of Port Issol, West Side   1938
Oil on canvas   23 x 28"
Lent by Dr. and Mrs. James Jay, New York

Villa Marie-Jeanne   1938
Oil on canvas   23¾ x 28¾"
Lent anonymously

Slanting Apple Tree   1938
Oil on canvas   23 x 28"
Lent by Mr. Chauncey L. Waddell, New York

Nude Figure Prone on Side   1939
Oil on canvas   23½ x 29"
Lent by Mr. and Mrs. Louis Sosland, Shawnee Mission, Kansas

Cottage Porch in Reflection   1940
Oil on canvas   15 x 21"
Lent by Mr. and Mrs. Robert A. Baldwin, Nashville, Tennessee

Shiloh   1940
Oil on canvas   36 x 32"
Lent by Commerce Trust Company, Foundation for Education in Fine Arts, Kansas City, Missouri

Constant   1941
Oil on canvas   23⅞ x 29"
Lent by Mr. Edwin Constant Dickinson, Tokyo, Japan

Ruin at Daphne   1943–53
Oil on canvas   48 x 60¼"
Lent by Metropolitan Museum of Art, New York
The Edward Joseph Gallagher III Memorial Collection, 1955

The Flag at Frazier's House   1947
Oil on canvas   12 x 10"
Lent by Ione and Hudson Walker, Forest Hills, New York

Self-Portrait   1949
Oil on canvas   23 x 20"
Lent by National Academy of Design, New York

*South Wellfleet Inn**   1950
Oil on canvas   33¼ x 43⅝"
Lent by Graham Gallery Ltd., New York

Rock, Cape Poge   1950
Oil on canvas   12 x 14½" (oval)
Lent by Mrs. Katherine White Reswick, Cleveland, Ohio

Carousel Bridge, Paris   1952
Oil on board   12 x 14½"
Lent by Bowdoin College Museum of Art, Brunswick, Maine

Windows, Paris   1952
Oil on canvas   12 x 16"
Lent by Mr. and Mrs. Gardner Jencks, New York

Window and Oar   1955
Oil on board   12 x 18"
Lent by Whitney Museum of American Art, New York

RICHARD DIEBENKORN

*Recollections of a Visit to Leningrad**   1965
Oil on canvas   73 x 84"
Lent by Poindexter Gallery, New York

Folding Chair   1966
Oil on canvas   51 x 48"
Lent by Poindexter Gallery, New York

Large Woman   1967
Oil on canvas   91 x 82"
Lent by Poindexter Gallery, New York

Window   1967
Oil on canvas   92 x 80"
Lent by Poindexter Gallery, New York

FRANK GALLO

The Critic 1964
Epoxy resin 13 x 11 x 13″
Lent by Mr. and Mrs. Leonard A. Lauder, New York

Man in Rocker 1965
Epoxy resin 40 x 32 x 13″
Lent by Mr. Milfred Tokoph, Highland Park, Illinois

Standing Beach Figure 1966
Epoxy resin 64½ x 17 x 11″
Lent by Gilman Gallery, Chicago, Illinois

Girl on Couch* 1967
Epoxy resin 48 x 51 x 40″
Lent by Graham Gallery Ltd., New York
Courtesy of the Museo de Bellas Artes, Caracas, Venezuela
The second cast, in the collection of the University of Nebraska,
will be shown at Washington, D.C. and Lincoln, Nebraska

RED GROOMS

City of Chicago* 1967
Installation of painted wood and paper with motorized parts
Components variable, dimensions variable
Lent by Allan Frumkin Gallery, Chicago, Illinois, in collaboration with
Tibor de Nagy Gallery, New York

JAMES McGARRELL

Divers 1963
Oil on canvas 94 x 81″
Lent by Indiana University Fine Arts Museum, Bloomington, Indiana
Gift of Joseph Cantor

Double Corner 1966
Oil on canvas 72 x 60″
Lent by Galerie Claude Bernard, Paris

Rainbow* 1967
Oil on canvas 92 x 77″
Lent by Mr. and Mrs. Douglass Boshkoff, Bloomington, Indiana

Two-part Inventions† 1965
Eight prints from suite of fifteen black and white lithographs with colophon
paper size : 26¾ x 21½″
Copy No. 41, printed by Imp. Clot. Bramsen et Georges, Paris, France
Lent by the artist

REUBEN NAKIAN

(Dimensions do not include the base)

Trojan Woman   1960–62
Plaster for bronze   109 x 62 x 30"
Lent by Egan Gallery, New York

Olympia   1961
Bronze   72 x 74 x 34"
Lent by Whitney Museum of American Art, New York
Gift of the Friends of the Whitney Museum

Birth of Venus   1963–66
Plaster for bronze   96 x 131 x 66"
Lent by Egan Gallery, New York

Goddess of the Golden Thighs   1964–65
Plaster for bronze   108 x 150 x 48"
Lent by Egan Gallery, New York

Judgment of Paris : Venus   1964–65
Plaster for bronze   81 x 88 x 60"
Lent by Egan Gallery, New York

Judgment of Paris : Minerva   1965–66
Plaster for bronze   97 x 83 x 50"
Lent by Egan Gallery, New York
First cast in the collection of Mr. B. E. Bensinger, Highland Park, Illinois

Hiroshima   1966
Plaster for bronze   111 x 72 x 48"
Lent by Egan Gallery, New York
First cast in the collection of the Museum of Modern Art, New York

*The Dance of Death : Herod**   1966–67
Plaster for bronze   102 x 76 x 63"
Lent by Egan Gallery, New York

*The Dance of Death : Salomé**   1966–67
Plaster for bronze   96 x 72 x 42"
Lent by Egan Gallery, New York

*The Dance of Death : Herodias**   1966–67
Plaster for bronze   105 x 57 x 39"
Lent by Egan Gallery, New York

FAIRFIELD PORTER

*The Pear Tree** 1962
Oil on canvas 75 x 60"
Lent by Tibor de Nagy Gallery, New York

Living Room 1964
Oil on canvas 60 x 48"
Lent by Mrs. Constance C. Jewett, New York

View of the Harbor 1965
Oil on canvas 45 x 45"
Lent by Mr. and Mrs. Wade Perry, New Haven, Connecticut

Columbus Day 1966
Oil on canvas 80 x 80"
Lent by Tibor de Nagy Gallery, New York

The following list of recently published books contains material pertinent to the scope of this exhibition References to the work of specific artists are included in the biographical sections.

Baur, John I. H. *Revolution and Tradition in Modern American Art*. Cambridge, Massachusetts, Harvard University Press, 1951

———. (ed.). *New Art in America*. Greenwich, Connecticut, New York Graphic Society, 1957 (see Dickinson)

Canaday, John. *Embattled Critic*. New York, Noonday Press, 1962 (see Baskin)

Chaet, Bernard. *Artists at Work*. Cambridge, Massachusetts, Webb Books, Inc., 1960 (see Baskin)

Feldman, Edmund B. *Art as Image and Idea*. Englewood Cliffs, New Jersey, Prentice-Hall, Inc., 1967 (see Baskin, Cremean, Diebenkorn, Gallo, Grooms, Nakian)

Geldzahler, Henry. *American Painting in the 20th Century*. New York, The Metropolitan Museum of Art, 1965 (see Dickinson)

Henning, Edward B. *Fifty Years of Modern Art: 1916–1966*. Cleveland, Ohio, Cleveland Museum of Art, 1966 (see Dickinson, Diebenkorn)

Kuh, Katharine. *The Artist's Voice: Talks with Seventeen Artists*. New York, Harper and Row, 1962 (see Dickinson)

Lippard, Lucy R. *Pop Art*. New York, Frederick A. Praeger, Inc., 1966 (see Grooms)

Rodman, Selden. *Conversations with Artists*. New York, Capricorn Books, 1961 (see Baskin)

———. *The Insiders*. Baton Rouge, Louisiana State University Press, 1960 (see Baskin, Dickinson)

Rose, Barbara. *American Art Since 1900: A Critical History*. New York, Frederick A. Praeger, Inc., 1967 (see Dickinson, Diebenkorn, Grooms, Nakian, Porter)

Selz, Peter. *New Images of Man*. New York, The Museum of Modern Art, 1959 (see Baskin, Diebenkorn, McGarrell)

Weller, Allen S. and Nordness, Lee (eds.). *Art U.S.A. Now*. New York, The Viking Press, 1963 (see Dickinson, Diebenkorn)

Photography

Baskin: O. E. Nelson; Walter Rosenblum (portrait and others)

Burford: Brenwasser; Jonas Dovydenas; Joan Liffringzug (portrait)

Cremean: Bard Clow (portrait and others); Henry Kahn; John F. Thompson

Dickinson: Rudolph Burckhardt; Geoffrey Clements; Peter A. Juley (portrait and others); Museum of Fine Arts, Springfield; O. E. Nelson; Photo Science Studio, Cornell University; Nathan Rabin; Kaz Tada; George Yater

Diebenkorn: Henry Kahn; The Pennsylvania Academy of the Fine Arts; VIB, University of Texas; Herb Weitman (portrait)

Gallo: Lee Balterman; Ferdinand Boesch; Bill Peterson (portrait)

Grooms: Jonas Dovydenas; George Drick (portrait)

McGarrell: Indiana University. Stephen Pressler (portrait)

Nakian: Thor Bostrom (portrait and others); G. D. Hackett; O. E. Nelson; Nathan Rabin

Porter: Ellen Auerbach; O. E. Nelson; Newsweek-Tony Rollo (portrait)